28/10   30p

Values for Living

TONY CAMPOLO

WORD
BOOKS

WORD BOOKS
Nelson Word Ltd
Milton Keynes, England
WORD AUSTRALIA
Kilsyth, Australia
WORD COMMUNICATIONS LTD
Vancouver, B.C., Canada
STRUIK CHRISTIAN BOOKS (PTY) LTD
Cape Town, South Africa
JOINT DISTRIBUTORS SINGAPORE —
ALBY COMMERCIAL ENTERPRISES PTE LTD
and
CAMPUS CRUSADE, ASIA LTD
PHILIPPINE CAMPUS CRUSADE FOR CHRIST
Quezon City, Philippines
CHRISTIAN MARKETING NEW ZEALAND LTD
Havelock North, New Zealand
JENSCO LTD
Hong Kong
SALVATION BOOK CENTRE
Malaysia

ISBN 0-85009-680-4 (Australia 1-86258-346-3)

Unless otherwise indicated, Scripture quotations are from the New International Version (NIV), © 1973, 1978, 1984 by International Bible Society.
Other Scripture quotations are from the following sources:
The New American Standard Bible (NASB), © 1960, 1962, 1963, 1968, 1971, 1972, 1973, 1975, 1977 the Lockman Foundation.
The Authorised Version of the Bible (AV).
New King James Version of the Bible (NKJV).

The quotations in the following studies are all used by permission.
Study 2 from *Holiness and the Spirit of the Age*, by Floyd McClung, © Floyd McClung. Nelson Word Ltd.
Study 3 from *Day by Day with C.H. Spurgeon*, compiled by Al Bryant, © 1980 Al Bryant. Nelson Word Ltd.
Studies 4,16 from *Why Settle for More and Miss the Best?* by Tom Sine, © 1987 Tom Sine. Nelson Word Ltd.
Studies 5,30 from *Growing Strong in the Seasons of Life*, by Charles R. Swindoll, © 1983 Charles R. Swindoll Inc. Zondervan Publishing House.
Study 6 from *Risky Living*, by Jamie Buckingham, © 1976 Logos International. Kingsway Publications Ltd./USA and Philippines Bridge Publishing.
Study 8 from *The Best of A.W. Tozer*, compiled by Warren Wiersbe, © 1978 Baker Book House Company, USA. Crossway Books.
Study 9 from *Celebration of Discipline*, by Richard J. Foster, © 1978 Richard J. Foster. Hodder and Stoughton Ltd./USA and Canada HarperCollins Publishers.
Study 10 from *Seven Wonders of the Spiritual World*, by Bill Hybels, © 1988 Bill Hybels. Nelson Word Ltd.
Study 11 from *A Force in the Earth*, by David Shibley, © 1989 David Shibley. Nelson Word Ltd.
Study 13 from *Flirting with the World*, by John White, © 1982 John White. Hodder and Stoughton Ltd./USA, Philippines and Canada Harold Shaw Publishers, Wheaton, IL.
Study 15 from *The Business of Heaven*, by C.S. Lewis, © 1984 C.S. Lewis Pte Ltd. Collins Fount Paperbacks.
Study 16 from *Eighth Day of Creation*, by Elisabeth O'Connor, © 1971. Nelson Word Ltd.
Study 17 from *Working for God*, by Ralph Turner, © Frontier Publishing International Ltd., 1993. Nelson Word Ltd.
Study 18 from *Life in the Spirit*, by D. Martyn Lloyd-Jones, © 1973 D.M. Lloyd-Jones. The Banner of Truth Trust.
Study 19 from *Issues Facing Christians Today*, by John Stott, © John Stott, 1984 and 1990. HarperCollins Publishers.
Study 20 from *Keeping your Kids Christian*, edited by Marshall Shelley, © 1990 Marshall Shelley. Nelson Word Ltd.
Study 21 from *How to be a Hero to your Kids*, by Josh McDowell and Dick Day, © 1991 Josh McDowell and Dick Day. Nelson Word Ltd.
Study 22 from *What happens when we Pray for our Families*, by Evelyn Christenson, © 1992. Scripture Press Foundation (UK) Ltd./USA and Philippines SP Publications Inc.
Study 23 from *Great Quotes and Illustrations*, compiled by George Sweeting, © 1985. Nelson Word Ltd.
Study 24 from *The Good Life*, by Max Anders, © 1993 Word Publishing. Nelson Word Ltd.
Study 26 from *Strength for the Day*, Daily Meditations with F.B. Meyer, © 1979 Word Inc. Nelson Word Ltd.
Study 27 from *The Gospel According to St. Mark*, An Introduction and Commentary, by R.A. Cole, © Inter-Varsity Press, London.
Study 28 from *Spiritual Disciplines for the Christian Life*, by Donald S Whitney, © 1991 Donald S. Whitney. Scripture Press Foundation (UK) Ltd./USA and Philippines NavPress.
Study 29 from *Through the Year with Watchman Nee*, © Harry Foster 1977, Kingsway Publications Ltd.
Study 31 from *Living above the Level of Mediocrity*, by Charles R. Swindoll, © 1987 Charles R. Swindoll. Nelson Word Ltd.

Created, designed and typeset by Frontier Publishing International Ltd., BN43 6RE, England. *Reproduced, printed and bound in Great Britain for* Nelson Word Ltd. *by* Ghyllprint Ltd., Heathfield.
94 95 96 97 / 10 9 8 7 6 5 4 3 2 1

Making the most of the studies ...

Welcome

Welcome to the Oasis study entitled *Values for Living*. Moses prayed, 'Teach us to number our days aright, that we may gain a heart of wisdom' (Ps. 90:12). He wanted to find out what would really satisfy him and to live for it.

2 days equals 2 months

We suggest that you take two days to cover each study and therefore two months to complete the book. You might want to work through the material more quickly, but if you take your time you are likely to benefit more. We recommend that you use the New International Version of the Bible (post-1983 version). The important thing is not that you finish fast, but that you hear from God *en route*! So aim to learn well and steadily build the teaching into your life.

Examine your values

Modern society argues that we get the most out of life by living for self. It encourages us to make as much money as possible, to spend it on whatever we fancy and to enjoy as many physical pleasures as we can. In stark contrast, Jesus tells us that if we want to be really happy, we will be meek, thirsty for righteousness and merciful to others. We show by our conduct which value system we have adopted and are living for.

Using some excellent illustrations, Tony Campolo challenges us to reflect on our lives, to risk more and to do more things that will live on after us. He suggests how we can inject life into our jobs, homes and church, and touches on subjects like prosperity preaching, helpful family rituals, fun among believers and the joy of Christian service.

The three sections under the main text relate to the teaching material. You may be asked to consider some aspect of the Christian life, to write down an answer, or to do something practical. The questions have been designed to help you to escape from legalism and to enjoy a deeper intimacy with the Holy Spirit. Let the Scripture verses inspire you in your walk with God.

Build a storehouse

The Bible says, 'Wise men store up knowledge' (Prov. 10:14), and Jesus underlines this when He calls us to '[bring] good things out of the good stored up in [our] heart' (Luke 6:45).

God wants to encourage and inform you through His Word. That's what the 'Food for thought' section is all about. It gives you the invaluable opportunity to hear direct from God and to store up what He says to you. **Please use a separate notebook** particularly for this section. Not only will it help you to crystallise your thoughts, but it will also be of tremendous reference value in the future.

As you study, refuse to let time pressurise you. Pray that God will speak to you personally and expect Him to do so. You may sometimes find that you're so enthralled by what He says to you that you're looking up many Scriptures which are not even suggested!

Finally, may God bless you as you work through this book. Discover for yourself how much more satisfying it is to adopt His value system than that of the world.

Have fun

This Oasis study guide is about adopting right values so that we can enjoy life to the full. Without fun, marriages don't work; jobs become intolerable and dehumanising; children are heartbreaking and religion becomes a drag. When life is not fun, it is hard to be spiritual.

People don't know how to have fun. Once when I was in Disneyland, I saw a woman shaking her little boy and screaming at him, 'you wanted to come, and now you're going to have fun whether you like it or not!'

It seems to me that too many people are just like that little boy. They force themselves to do things that are supposed to be fun, but feel like crying. They acquire what they think they want in life, then find that this 'heart's desire' fails to deliver the gratifications promised. When you ask them how things are going, they say, 'Couldn't be better.' But you sense that perhaps they couldn't be worse.

When I was a boy, a friend and I talked about what might happen if we broke into a store and changed all the price tags. We imagined what it would be like the next morning when people came into the store and discovered that say, matches were more expensive than radios!

▓ To consider

Look up the word 'fun' in a dictionary and write down what it says.

_____

_____

How do you think Christians have fun?

_____

_____

▓ To meditate on

God wants us to enjoy life.
'To the man who pleases him, God gives ... happiness' (Eccl. 2:26).
'I have come that they may have life, and have it to the full' (John 10:10).
'Remain in my love ... I have told you this so that my joy may be in you and that your joy may be complete' (John 15:9,11).
'God ... richly provides us with everything for our enjoyment' (1 Tim. 6:17).

Sometimes I think that Satan has played the same kind of trick on all of us. He has broken into our lives and changed the price tags on things. Too often, under the influence of his malicious ploy, we treat what deserves to be treated with loving care as though it were of little worth. On the other hand, we find ourselves tempted to make great sacrifices for what, in the long run of life, has no lasting value and delivers very little gratification.

How can we have fun when we don't know what is important; when we ignore the things that God has designed to deliver His joy; when we give our lives to the things He warned would only make us sad?

If we are to be fun people, we must put first things first. We must give attention to those things that foster good family life, satisfying work patterns, positive church life, and viable personal relationships. We must give our time and energies to things that God teaches us to value, and organise our lives around things essential to life as He wants it to be lived. In other words, if we are to get the most out of life, we have to get our values straightened out. That is what this book is all about.

➤ Look up the following Scriptures and write down what God wants His people to enjoy.

Nehemiah 8:10;
Psalms 37:3,11,18,19;
Proverbs 13:2; 28:16;
Isaiah 3:10;
Jeremiah 33:6;
Acts 2:4;
Ephesians 6:2,3.

➤ Read Romans 12:2.

➤ Where do people get the idea that doing God's will is wearisome?

▓ To question

What three things do you spend most time doing when you are free?

_____

_____

Would you say that your life was fun? Give reasons.

_____

_____

The presence of 'fun' will make a significant impact on everything you do. I believe that the only things healthy people do and continue to do are those things that are *fun*.
Steve Sjogren
Equipping the Saints magazine,
Spring 1993

Conflicting values

Do not love the world or anything in the world. If anyone loves the world, the love of the Father is not in him. For everything in the world — the cravings of sinful man, the lust of his eyes and the boasting of what he has and does — comes not from the Father but from the world. The world and its desires pass away, but the man who does the will of God lives for ever (1 John 2:15–17).

Jesus tells us in the Beatitudes how we can be happy. But today's young people would scorn this teaching. It opposes everything that they think will bring them fun in life.

According to Jesus, the happiest people are those who become poor as they respond to the needs of others. But the 'yuppie' generation argues that happiness results from gaining financial success for self.

Jesus taught that those who are happiest empathise with the sufferings of others. But young people tend to think that happiness can best be found by focusing on their well-being and not worrying about the heartbreak of those outside their personal world.

Whereas Jesus called meek people happy, yuppies believe that happiness comes through a go-getting, success-seeking attitude which leaves little regard for loyalty to others.

Jesus' teaching about purity of heart must seem hopelessly naïve to today's youth! They believe in 'Number One' and are geared up for personal gratification and sexual pleasure.

Their commitment to success at all costs makes them somewhat merciless towards those whose personal limitations thwart their

▓ To pray

How would you recognise a worldly Christian?

_____

_____

Pray for 'worldly Christians' in your local church.

Pray also that Christians in general will seek Christ's value system rather than turn aside to the worldly alternative.

▓ To meditate on

God calls us to live for Him.
'What good is it for a man to gain the world world, yet forfeit his soul?' (Mark 8:36)
'God said to him, "You fool! This very night your life will be demanded from you. Then who will get what you have prepared for yourself?"' (Luke 12:20)
'The man who loves his life will lose it, while the man who hates his life in this world will keep it for eternal life' (John 12:25).

dreams. They believe that people get what they deserve and that those who fall by the wayside warrant little attention from those who have the talent and make the sacrifices essential for personal achievement. What Jesus says about being merciful must seem like sentimentalism.

Jesus told us that peacemaking brings happiness, but they believe that the world is basically a jungle and only those who have the instinct to compete for survival can live in it.

Yuppies are interested in having good reports on their accomplishments and are unwilling to be 'persecuted for righteousness' sake'. The idea of opposing unjust practices seems crazy when such stands elicit negative responses from those in positions of power and influence.

Are they churchgoers? Maybe. But they hardly possess a Christian value system.

When fifty people aged 95+ were asked, 'If you could live your life again, what would you do differently?' three answers constantly re-emerged: 'I'd reflect more; I'd risk more; I'd do more things that would live on after I'm dead.'

I am convinced that people who want to have fun would do well to consider the observations of those whom time has made wise.

▒ To consider

How would you reply if you were asked, 'If you could live your life again, what would you do differently?'

_____

_____

_____

_____

_____

▒ Food for thought

➢ Read Matthew 5:3–12 and write down in a notebook what you understand by each beatitude.

➢ Compare your life with what you have written.

➢ On a single sheet of paper, write down how you need to change and put the paper in a prominent place where you can refer to it often.

When we absorb the values of the culture which surrounds us, how can we be separate from it? Holiness does not call us to get more *out* of life, but to put more of ourselves *into* life. Holiness means that we are set free from the cycle of inwardness and self-awareness and set apart from the world. Holiness means that we can live a life that resists the spirit of the age. Holiness sets the Christian free to live above the fads of fulfillment and see the Person who personifies life itself.
Floyd McClung

I'd reflect more

For the grace of God that brings salvation has appeared to all men. It teaches us to say 'No' to ungodliness and worldly passions, and to live self-controlled, upright and godly lives in this present age, while we wait for the blessed hope — the glorious appearing of our great God and Saviour, Jesus Christ, who gave himself for us to redeem us from all wickedness and to purify for himself a people that are his very own, eager to do what is good (Titus 2:11–14).

The elderly people in Study 2 realised in retrospect that they had not paid proper attention to the most important things. We need to reflect on our lives now, otherwise we may fail to experience many of the blessings that God wants us to enjoy.

Sometimes we can be too casual about our salvation. We speak about Jesus' taking our punishment but fail to consider the magnitude of His sacrifice. If we reflected more on the price He paid, our lives would be very different.

While Jesus' suffering at Calvary was a once and for all event, He still experiences pain when we continue to sin. If we reflected on how much our sin hurt Jesus, we would give it up and earnestly pursue righteousness.

I once knew a woman whose husband paid her little attention. She lacked self-worth and became suicidal. Then she got to know a young widower. This new man in her life found her interesting, treated her as though she were still physically attractive and made her feel alive again. Not surprisingly, the relationship developed into an extended extramarital affair.

When she told me about her lover, she showed no remorse or guilt. She explained that

▩ To pray

Pray for individuals who have slipped into sin.

Pray also that God will help the leaders in your church to resist the temptation to sin.

▩ To meditate on

Salvation brings joy.
'Rejoice that your names are written in heaven' (Luke 10:20).
'You believe in him and are filled with an inexpressible and glorious joy, for you are receiving the goal of your faith, the salvation of your souls' (1 Pet. 1:8,9).
'(He) is able to keep you from falling and to present you before his glorious presence without fault and with great joy' (Jude v. 24).

her husband was detached from her and had not responded to her pleas for intimacy for years, and that her children had moved away and seldom contacted her. She informed me that she and her lover were very careful about their meetings and that there was almost no likelihood of their being found out.

'He makes me feel wonderful about myself and I help to meet some of his needs,' she told me. 'Nobody's hurt. Nobody suffers.'

'What about Jesus?' I replied. 'Do you ever think that what you are doing causes Him to suffer?' She could tolerate her sin only because she did not reflect more on His pain. Reflection would have driven her to repentance.

Sometimes, when life is overbearing, one of the few routes to joy lies in reflecting on our new standing in Christ. The Bible tells us that not only does Jesus take our sin and make it His own, He also gives us all His righteousness. God views us as being as wonderful as His Son.

When I think about this, I often experience a 'high'. I see myself bounding into heaven and boldly marching up to the throne to meet my heavenly Father. Joy comes through reflecting on glory. Let's reflect on it from time to time.

▓ To reflect

Reflect on your life and write down what God shows you.

_____

_____

_____

Reflect on the life to come.

Spend 10 minutes praising God for reserving you a place in eternity.

Grace and glory always go together. God has married them, and none can divorce them. The Lord will never deny a soul glory to whom he has freely given grace. Glory, the glory of heaven, the glory of eternity, the glory of Jesus, the glory of the Father, the Lord will surely give to His chosen. Oh, rare promise of a faithful God!
C.H. Spurgeon

Reflect on life

Emily is the main character in Thornton Wilder's play, *Our Town*. When she dies, the spirits in the afterlife grant her one wish and she chooses to go back in time and watch herself and her family on her twelfth birthday.

As an invisible observer, she is dismayed by what she sees and hears. Neither she nor her family seem to give serious attention to each other. They appear casual, fail to interact emotionally and waste what she now knows to be infinitely precious time. She is shocked that they live with so little reflection on life's importance. Then she turns to the audience and asks, 'Do any of you ever really live life while you're living it?'

Most people I know are so detached from life that they seem to be in a trance which renders them more dead than alive. And they sleepwalk their way through life without much awareness of the wonder of it.

Those elderly people wished that their eyes had been more open to what many might call the simple pleasures of life. One of them wished he had taken more baths and fewer showers. He said, 'I just didn't spend enough time experiencing how good a hot bath really feels.'

▨ To do

From today on, make a conscious effort to 'live life while you're living it'. How could you use your senses (i.e. sight, hearing etc.) more effectively?

_____

_____

_____

_____

▨ To meditate on

We must learn to live life now.
'The bread of God is he who comes down from heaven and gives life to the world' (John 6:33).
'Whoever believes in me ... streams of living water will flow from within him' (John 7:38).
'For to me, to live is Christ and to die is gain' (Phil. 1:21).
'He ... sent his one and only Son into the world that we might live through him' (1 John 4:9).

As I reflect on my own life, I note that ever since I was filled with the Spirit, I have had an exuberant awareness of the specialness and wonder of life, and that awareness invigorates me wildly. Often, my enthusiasm expresses itself in ways that are seldom considered 'religious' in a formal sense. Yet I believe they are the essence of what religion is all about.

Clowning around is part of living just as much as crying. I can accept both. What I cannot accept is that 'deadness' in people which renders them incapable of either passionate joy or agonising sorrow — a lifestyle that is 'neither hot nor cold'.

Jesus has much more to offer us than deliverance from hell and the promise of heaven sometime in the future. He wants us to have life 'more abundantly' here and now.

When we become Christians something wonderful happens. Jesus becomes a living presence within us and gives us a dynamic new sense of aliveness. This equips us to appreciate life's experiences with a more joyful intensity than ever before.

If you were asked, 'Are you really living life while you're living it?' how would you reply?

■ To pray

Pray that God will help Christians to drop spiritual numbness and be excited about life.

Name individuals who seem somewhat too sober and ask God to break into their lives and give them a new sense of fun.

_____

_____

_____

■ Food for thought

➤ Meditate through Psalm 98, noting that the Psalmist looks back in time, praises God now, and looks forward to Jesus' return.

➤ Apply these past, present and future aspects to yourself.

For example:

- When the Psalm mentions 'marvellous things', recall some marvellous things that God has done for you in the past.

- When the Psalm calls for praise, do that as enthusiastically as it suggests.

- When the Psalm anticipates Jesus' return, express your longing to be with Him in heaven.

Most Christians ... tend to stay within the safe shores of the familiar, regardless of whether this strategy brings the desired outcome ... But a growing number ... are bursting out of the confining conventional boxes with which they have been raised — discovering the delight of creating a much broader array of ways to seek first the purposes of God ... they are having the time of their lives.
Tom Sine

I'd risk more

(Deborah) ... said to
(Barak), 'The LORD ...
commands you: "Go,
take with you ten
thousand men ... and
lead the way to Mount
Tabor. I will lure Sisera ...
with his chariots and his
troops to the Kishon
River and give him into
your hands."' Barak
said to her, 'If you go
with me, I will go; but if
you don't go with me, I
won't go.' 'Very well,'
Deborah said ... 'But
because of the way
you are going about
this, the honour will not
be yours, for the LORD
will hand Sisera over to
a woman'
(Judg. 4:6–9).

R isk-taking is exciting. It convinces that you've got what it takes to break out of the mould which society casts for you. When the elderly people who were surveyed looked back, they didn't think much about their successes or failures. What seemed to matter more were the risks they had taken.

Some people hate their jobs. They live in quiet desperation, knowing neither the thrill of victory nor the agony of defeat. Joy evades them and they survive by detaching themselves from what they do and fantasising about being elsewhere. They know what's happening, but haven't got what it takes to launch out into something dangerously new.

When I ask such people what they would really like to do, their faces light up. They brim with excitement as they describe the glorious plans that they have in mind. But when I question, 'Why not do it?' their faces drop and the excuses come. They repress their dreams because they are afraid to take the risks.

Moses sent twelve men to spy out Canaan. When they returned, ten of them said that it would be foolhardy to challenge the giants who lived there. They were afraid to take the risks

▓ To risk

Take some risks that are not characteristic of you (e.g. pray aloud at the prayer meeting, speak to someone you don't know, visit an elderly person, invite someone round for a meal, coffee, etc.).

▓ To meditate on

Risk must be accompanied by faith.
'"Lord, if it's you," Peter replied, "tell me to come to you on the water." "Come," he said. Then Peter got down out of the boat' (Matt. 14:28,29).
'Everything that does not come from faith is sin' (Rom. 14:23).
'Without faith it is impossible to please God ... through faith (they) conquered kingdoms, administered justice, and gained what was promised'
(Heb. 11:6,33).

involved in entering the land that God had set aside for them.

On the other hand, Joshua and Caleb, who had also seen the giants, wanted to go for it. They were willing to challenge the odds to live out a dream. For such risk takers, there is always a promised land.

Certainly, failure is a possibility, and if you fail, you will be mocked. But does that matter? The promised land belongs to the person who takes the risks, whose face is marred with dust and sweat, who strives valiantly while daring everything, who may err and fall, but who has done his or her best. This person's place shall never be with those cold and timid individuals who know neither victory nor defeat.

If only I could persuade timid souls I meet to listen to that inner voice of the Spirit, which challenges us to attempt great things for God and expect great things from Him. If only I could inspire them to heed that inner urging that tells them, 'Go for it!' I cannot say what people should do with their lives, but I can say what they should not do. No one should devote his or her life to safety, to a course of action that offers no challenge and no fun.

▓ To consider

Where do you want to be in five years' time?

_____

How are you making progress towards that goal?

_____

Prayerfully consider whether God is calling you into something new. If so, check this out with a church leader.

Far better it is to dare mighty things, to win glorious triumphs, even though checkered by failure, than to take rank with those poor spirits who neither enjoy much nor suffer much because they live in the gray twilight that knows neither victory nor defeat.
Teddy Roosevelt

Launch out

'And now the cry of the Israelites has reached me, and I have seen the way the Egyptians are oppressing them. So now, go. I am sending you to Pharaoh to bring my people the Israelites out of Egypt.' But Moses said to God, 'Who am I, that I should go to Pharaoh and bring the Israelites out ot Egypt?' (Exod. 3:9–11)

A small missionary organisation once interviewed people for the position of executive director of overseas operations. All the candidates loved Jesus and were highly qualified, but the successful applicant was chosen primarily because of the way in which he answered one question: 'Why do you want to do missionary work?'

He gave the expected responses about serving others for Christ. Then he said simply, 'I have to admit that one of the main reasons is because it's fun.' That did it. The interviewers couldn't help but be attracted to a candidate who could have fun in the midst of all the hardships that would go with the job, someone who would get a kick out of serving others.

Many Christians think only young people are called to the mission field, or to do some daring work on the home front. But the call to live dangerously for God is for all. You're never too old to do great things for the Kingdom.

Abraham was 75 years old when he left Haran. Imagine his waking up one morning and declaring to 65 year old Sarah, 'I've just had a vision. God is going to create a new nation through us.' Maybe she laughed. As

▓ To do

Write down the names of three Bible characters who took risks for God. Give reasons for your choice.

_____

_____

_____

_____

_____

▓ To meditate on

We need to press on.
'I press on to take hold of that for which Christ Jesus took hold of me ... I press on towards the goal to win the prize for which God has called me heaven-wards in Christ Jesus' (Phil. 3:12,14).
'We are not of those who shrink back ... but of those who believe' (Heb. 10:39).
'Let us throw off everything that hinders and the sin that so easily entangles, and let us run with perseverance the race marked out for us' (Heb. 12:1).

they left home, it is possible that they had this conversation with their neighbours:

Neighbours:	Where are you going?
Abraham:	Don't know.
Neighbours:	What are you going to be doing?
Abraham:	Don't know that either.
Neighbours:	Then why are you leaving?
Abraham:	Because God gave me a vision.

If God gives you a vision, will you dismiss it as impossible, or run with it?

Not only does God want us to take risks with our vocations, He also wants us to take risks in our relationships. Many Christians feel lonely. But often that loneliness stems from a fear of reaching out to others. In the absence of such daring, the paralysing terror of rejection takes over. Of course, people can rebuff our efforts to be friendly. But if we do not risk rejection, we will inevitably be lonely.

Jesus can help us take the risks that make friendships possible. If we seek to live close to Him, He will show us how incredibly precious we are, and this knowledge will give us a strong sense of self-worth. Once our identities are established in God, we will reach out to others in love regardless of the risks involved.

▓ To consider

How do you react when you feel overlooked or rejected?

_____

_____

How do you think you should react?

_____

_____

Reach out to someone who might be feeling 'left out' this week.

▓ Food for thought

➢ Although the work of God is hard, it is immensely satisfying, even enjoyable.

➢ Read through Psalm 119 and underline all the verses which suggest that David actually enjoyed not just reading, but obeying God's laws.

➢ Can you identify with his enthusiasm for living as God desired?

➢ What is God saying to you through this Psalm?

The most exciting and whole people I know are those who leave the comforts and security of home, who turn their backs on well-paying jobs and worldly fame to go to the remote areas of the earth as missionary doctors, pilots, translators, and teachers. Many of them die on foreign soil, unrecognised by men. But the price of death is very small when compared to what they purchase by their risky living. After all, what's the use of living if you don't attempt the impossible.
Jamie Buckingham

I'd do more that lived on

'How the mighty have fallen in battle in battle! Jonathan lies slain on your heights. I grieve for you, Jonathan my brother; you were very dear to me. Your love for me was wonderful, more wonderful than that of women' (2 Sam. 1:25,26).

The fifty elderly people said that if they could live life over again, they would do more things that would live on after they were dead. Every human being wants to do something of worth that will have lasting significance.

When we draw near to death, we become aware of the importance of leaving something good behind. That is why young people give little thought to the significance of their lives, while the elderly think about it all the time.

On the last Sunday of the year we ask the students in our church to report on their educational experiences. Since ours is a Black Baptist Church, the older members have not had the opportunities that the young people enjoy and love to hear what their children and grandchildren are learning.

One such Sunday, after about six students had given their reports, my pastor delivered some closing words. 'Children,' he said, 'you're going to die! When you were born, you alone were crying and everybody else was happy. The important question I want to ask is this: When you die are you alone going to be happy, leaving everybody else crying. The answer depends on whether you live to get titles or testimonies.

▨ To pray

Read Acts 9:36–43.

Pray that when you die, you will have a similar effect on others as Dorcas had.

▨ To meditate on

Love excels over knowledge. 'Knowledge puffs up, but love builds up. The man who thinks he knows something does not yet know as he ought to know. But the man who loves God is known by God' (1 Cor. 8:1–3). 'If I have the gift of prophecy and can fathom all mysteries and all knowledge, and if I have a faith that can move mountains, but have not love, I am nothing' (1 Cor. 13:2). 'Do everything in love' (1 Cor. 16:14).

'When they lay you in the grave, are people going to list your degrees and awards or give testimonies of the blessing you were to them? There's nothing wrong with title, but if it ever comes down to a choice between a title or a testimony, go for the testimony.'

He then went through the Bible citing individuals who had power and prestige, and people whose lives were characterised by loving service. He rhythmically shouted his sermon, each line stronger than the one before:

Pharaoh may have had the title ...
But Moses had the testimony!
Nebuchadnezzar may have had the title ...
But Daniel had the testimony!
Queen Jezebel may have had the title ...
But Elijah had the testimony!'

He kept this up, hammering away at the contrasts. When he reached the climax of his message he screamed, 'Pilate may have had the title' — then he paused for what seemed like an eternity — 'But my Jesus had the testimony!'

Will you leave behind a newspaper column telling everyone how important you were, or will you leave people who give testimonies of how they've lost the best friend they ever had?

▓ Food for thought

➤ Read 1 Corinthians 3:11–15.

➤ Divide a piece of paper in half.

- On the left, describe someone who is building with 'gold, silver or costly stones'.

- On the right, describe someone who is building with 'wood, hay or straw'.

➤ Don't allow yourself to be condemned, but let the Holy Spirit point out areas in your life where your testimony could be improved.

▓ To consider

Ask someone who is close to you how he/she would remember you if you died tomorrow.

How would you like to be remembered?

_____

_____

What improvements could you make now?

_____

_____

I want to build with silver and gold in my generation.
I want to build with silver and gold while I am alive.
I want to give my life for something that will last forever.
Mark Altrogge
In my Generation,
© 1982 People of Destiny Int/Word Music Inc/Word Music (UK) Copy Care Ltd.

Testimony or title?

'Let your light shine before men, that they may see your good deeds and praise your Father in heaven' (Matt. 5:16).

Live such good lives among the pagans that, though they accuse you of doing wrong, they may see your good deeds and glorify God on the day he visits us (1 Pet. 2:12).

My son, Bart, was an outstanding high school soccer player. He won a lot of trophies, set records as a goalie and carried himself with distinction whenever he played.

During his first year of high school he had to compete for the goalie position with a senior who, up until Bart's arrival, seemed assured of selection. But Bart beat him and started the first game of the season.

Joel, the senior player, must have been terribly disappointed and could easily have held a grudge. But he was a Christian. Instead of withdrawing from the team and turning against Bart, he became the team's best cheerleader and Bart's friend. Joel drove Bart to games, went to parties with him, and asked him to be part of the youth group at his church.

One Saturday Joel and Bart were away for several hours. When they got home Bart came into my study, sat down and said, 'Dad, I made an important decision this morning. Joel asked me to turn my life over to Jesus and I did.'

I had often talked to my son about Jesus and asked him to become a Christian. I had taken him to countless evangelistic meetings where he heard me preach the gospel and invite

▨ **To pray**

Consider your relationships with others. Are you a vibrant testimony to them?

Pray for God's help at being a more effective witness of Jesus.

Take every opportunity to tell others about Him.

▨ **To meditate on**

We must avoid bitterness and grudges. 'Do not seek revenge or bear a grudge against one of your people, but love your neighbour as yourself' (Lev. 19:18). 'Do not take revenge ... but leave room for God's wrath' (Rom. 12:19). 'Get rid of all bitterness' (Eph. 4:31). 'See to it that no-one misses the grace of God and that no bitter root grows up to cause trouble and defile many' (Heb. 12:15).

people to come to Christ. But Joel was able to get through to him when I could not.

I doubt if Joel could have done what he did if he had not backed up his verbal testimony with a living testimony. What Joel had to say would have carried little weight with my son if he had not demonstrated Christlikeness in the gracious way he treated Bart and reacted to the circumstances surrounding those soccer trials.

By the end of the soccer season, Bart had earned a lot of titles, but Joel had won himself a fantastic testimony. On that final day when we all stand before the Lord to be judged, I am sure that Bart's trophies and titles won't mean a thing. But I am also sure that he will be ready to give a testimony about the difference that Joel made to his life.

In doing the Christlike thing, Joel saved himself from what might have been a very long and painful school year. He could have been sullen and nasty over his displacement from the team. Instead, he had a great time, made a friend and sealed something that will last for eternity. Following Jesus delivered him from bitterness and opened up a relationship that gave him a lot of fun.

▓ To check

Read Genesis 50:15–21.

How do you think people reveal that they're nursing grudges against others?

_____

_____

_____

_____

Check your own heart.

▓ Food for thought

➤ Read Acts 6:3a,5; 8:4–24.

➤ Divide a sheet of paper in half. On the right, put the heading 'Philip' and on the left, 'Simon'.

➤ Using the relevant verses, list the differences between the characters and desires of the two men.

➤ Let the Holy Spirit speak to you.

I want deliberately to encourage this mighty longing after God. The lack of it has brought us to our present low estate. The stiff and wooden quality about our religious lives is a result of our lack of holy desire. Complacency is a deadly foe of all spiritual growth. Acute desire must be present or there will be no manifestation of Christ to His people. He waits to be wanted. Too bad that with many of us He waits so long, so very long, in vain.
A.W. Tozer

The small and the secret

'Whoever can be trusted with very little can also be trusted with much, and whoever is dishonest with very little will also be dishonest with much. So if you have not been trustworthy in handling worldly wealth, who will trust you with true riches? And if you have not been trustworthy with someone else's property, who will give you property of your own?' (Luke 16:10–12)

We all have a fascination with greatness. Sometimes it deludes us into thinking that we are significant only when we do something that results in public recognition. But really worthwhile deeds are often done quietly and attract no great publicity.

One day I was sitting on a plane when I noticed a stunning young woman across the aisle. After a few minutes a very macho-looking guy sat next to her. In no time he had her thoroughly involved in conversation. Then suddenly, she pulled a Bible from her shoulder bag and, with eyes sparkling, began telling him the way of salvation through Jesus.

When the plane landed, most of the people squeezed into the aisle, but the 'with it' guy and the gorgeous woman remained seated. Their heads were bowed in prayer as he accepted Christ as his Saviour.

That woman will not be granted a doctorate for what she did, nor will she be mentioned in the media. But her action will have eternal significance and will live on after she is dead.

Sometimes the most important things are done anonymously. I know a man who loves to use his money to help others, but they never

▓ To consider

Bearing in mind Jesus' assessment of 'greatness' how could you be 'greater'? Make practical suggestions.

_____

_____

_____

_____

_____

▓ To meditate on

Here is Jesus' idea of greatness. 'Whoever practises and teaches these commands will be called great in the kingdom of heaven' (Matt. 5:19). 'Whoever wants to become great among you must be your servant, and whoever wants to be first must be slave of all' (Mark 10:43,44). 'He who is least among you all — he is the greatest' (Luke 9:48).

know his identity. On one occasion I told him about a student who might have to drop out of Bible College because of lack of funds. The man paid the student's bills and he became a fine preacher who influenced thousands of lives.

Many individuals tuck their money away while they are living and leave it to those who don't need it when they die. They could sponsor candidates for the ministry or on the mission field, so why do they waste the opportunity?

Many Christians who give generously to Bible College students tell me how much joy it gives them. They watch the young people as they study, and after graduation, they sometimes visit the work and see the blessings that their gifts have made possible. What could people do with their money to give them greater pleasure?

Some of the most important things we do are often undramatic: sending cards, visiting the elderly, baby-sitting or phoning to encourage others. Once done, these things are quickly forgotten by those who do them, but often recalled by those whom they have blessed. On Judgement Day Jesus will reward a lot of people who can hardly remember the good deeds for which they will be honoured.

▓ To review

Review with God the way you use your finances.

Do you enjoy telling others about Christ? Should you? Pray about this.

▓ Food for thought

➢ Read Matthew 6:1–18. Look up the word 'hypocrite' in a dictionary and write down the definition in a notebook.

➢ Why is it hard to do 'acts of righteousness' in secret?

➢ Consider the way you give, pray and fast. Could you be more discreet? Be encouraged that as you do these things in secret, God *will* reward you. The word 'might' does not appear.

Self-righteous service requires external rewards. It needs to know that people see and appreciate the effort. It seeks human applause — with proper religious modesty of course. True service rests contented in hiddenness. It does not fear the lights and blare of attention, but it does not seek them either. Since it is living out of a new Center of Reference the divine nod of approval is completely sufficient.
Richard Foster

Things that last

'Defend the cause of
the weak and
fatherless; maintain the
rights of the poor and
oppressed. Rescue the
weak and needy;
deliver them from the
hand of the wicked'
(Ps. 82:3,4).

Blessed is he who is kind
to the needy
(Prov. 14:21).

At the beginning of every school year, a teacher called Miss Thompson used to tell her new pupils, 'Boys and girls, I have no favourites.' Sadly, she wasn't being completely truthful, because she didn't like Teddy Stallard.

Teddy didn't seem interested in school. He wore musty clothes, had unkempt hair and went round with a dead pan, blank expression. Miss Thompson got a perverse pleasure out of putting X's next to the wrong answers on his papers. She should have known better. His records said that he showed promise, but had a very poor home situation and received little interest or help from his parents. His mother died when he was in the third grade.

At Christmas time the boys and girls gave presents to Miss Thompson. When she opened Teddy's brown paper packet, out fell a gaudy rhinestone bracelet with half the stones missing, and a bottle of cheap perfume.

The boys and girls began to giggle and smirk, but Miss Thompson silenced them by putting on the bracelet and dabbing some of the scent on her wrist. Holding it up for all the other children to smell, she said, 'Doesn't it smell lovely?' and they readily agreed.

▓ To do

Ask God for opportunities to reach out to people who are not particularly likeable or attractive.

How could you do this?

_____

_____

_____

_____

▓ To meditate on

Let's continue to do good.
'Let us not become weary in doing good, for at the proper time we will reap a harvest if we do not give up. Therefore, as we have opportunity, let us do good to all people, especially to those who belong to the family of believers' (Gal. 6:9,10).
'Consider him who endured such opposition from sinful men, so that you will not grow weary and lose heart' (Heb. 12:3).

When everyone had gone home, Teddy came up to Miss Thompson's desk and said softly, 'Miss Thompson, you smell just like my mother — and her bracelet looks real pretty on you too. I'm glad you liked my presents.' When he left, she knelt and asked God to forgive her.

From then on she was committed to her children and did things for them that would live on after her. By the end of that school year, Teddy had showed dramatic improvement.

She didn't hear from him for a long time, then one day she received a note which said, 'I will be graduating second in my class'. Four years later, another note came — 'I will be graduating first in my class'. After another four years Teddy sent her the following letter:

'Dear Miss Thompson, As of today, I am Theodore Stallard, M.D. ... I wanted you to be the first to know. I am getting married next month ... I want you to come and sit where my mother would sit if she were alive. You are the only family I have now; Dad died last year.'

Miss Thompson went to that wedding and sat where Teddy's mother would have sat. She deserved to sit there; she had done something for Teddy that he could never forget.

▓ Food for thought

➢ Read James 2:1–13. In a notebook, write down some ways in which we can show favouritism (particularly the subtle ways that other people might not notice).

➢ Write down in the notebook what Jesus says about those who show favouritism.

➢ Ask Him to reveal to you any favouritism that you might be showing towards others.

➢ Break this habit today.

▓ To pray

Pray for people who work with children, e.g. teachers, Sunday School teachers, staff in children's homes or hospitals, etc.

Ask God to bless the children in your local church.

Ask God to reach out to children who are suffering from physical or sexual abuse.

Is it time you ... said, 'I want to be used to encourage and assist the afflicted and oppressed, and I want to be used to inform the world that sinners matter to God'? ... Just pray: 'I'm available, God. Please use me.'
Bill Hybels

Christians and work

W hy is it that the poor in the slums and on
the tenant farms of the USA appear
overwhelmed with despair, while the poor in the
slums of Latin America seem to have a real joy?
The answer may lie in the interpretation that
each group attaches to poverty.

The people of Latin America believe that
Jesus regards the poor as deserving of the
special blessing of God. But we in America or
the UK think that the rich are the blessed of
God while the poor are alienated from Him.

In modern America many TV evangelists
promise us that faithfulness to God brings
wealth and health. I have trouble with this kind
of message — probably because of my
experiences in Latin America and Africa where I
have met many desperately poor people whose
love for Jesus outshines mine. I have also seen
too many instances where the wicked prosper
while the righteous are oppressed.

Sadly, some Christians use this theology to
justify ignoring the poor. They argue that
people will never prosper economically until
they come to know Christ. Our job is to save
souls, not to waste time on improving social
conditions which will take care of themselves.

▓ To pray

Buy a newspaper, listen to a radio news
broadcast or watch the news on TV
and write down in a notebook some
present day examples of poverty.

Pray for the people you've just read
about, and for those who are trying to
help them.

▓ To meditate on

God calls us to reach out to the needy.
'Loose the chains of injustice ... set the
oppressed free ... share your food with
the hungry ... provide the poor
wanderer with shelter ... clothe (the
naked)' (Isa. 58:6,7).
'Sell your possessions and give to the
poor' (Luke 12:33).
'When you give a banquet, invite the
poor, the crippled, the lame, the blind,
and you will be blessed'
(Luke 14:13,14).

While I find their attitude selfish, I cannot completely discount what they say, since Christians do tend to translate their faith into creative economic productivity.

Several years ago, I visited a mountain village in Latin America where there was dishonesty; alcoholism; rampant unemployment and family breakdown. A few years later I returned and was amazed to note the clean streets and the industrious spirit among the people.

I was told that the changes were largely due to a Catholic priest who was baptised in the Spirit in the capital city. When he returned, he talked to people about his experience, and it wasn't long before half the village had been filled with the Spirit too. They turned from immorality and embraced hard work.

Christian conversion can have economic consequences, but not necessarily. In many places, believers who live righteously will still languish in deprivation because of that society's structural evil.

Wherever there are economic arrangements which reduce people to poverty, believers must act to change those arrangements and foster those traits that make for economic prosperity.

▨ To do

What practical things could you do to help the needy?

_____

_____

_____

_____

This week, send a letter to someone of influence about an issue which is concerning you, e.g. local sex shop, abortion, broadcasting standards, etc.

▨ Food for thought

➤ How can Christians reconcile Deuteronomy 28:1–14 with 2 Corinthians 6:3–10 and 9:6–11?

➤ If someone asked you for your opinion on the teaching that Christians should enjoy wealth and health, what would you say?

➤ What biblical support would you give to your answer?

The exciting irony of the Christian adventure is that under the new covenant we give to receive, we profit by losing, and we find our lives by laying them down. The follower of Jesus is first a producer, not a consumer. The follower's emphasis is serving, not being served. The disciple remembers the words of our Lord, 'It is more blessed to give than to receive' (Acts 20:35). World missionary advance is the why — and the redeeming social value — of the prosperity message.
David Shibley

Wanted: job enthusiasm

The Catholicism of the Middle Ages urged
people who really wanted to serve God to
leave their worldly vocations and go to convents
and monasteries. In contrast, the Reformers
(and particularly Calvin) argued that Christians
need not separate themselves from worldly
economic activities, but could serve God in
them. So if bakers, carpenters and farmers saw
their jobs as a primary way of serving God, they
could serve Him in their respective activities.

The Calvinists believed that dedicated
Christians would always work diligently, not
just when their employers were watching. The
products, they taught, should never evidence a
slipshod quality, because they were supposed
to glorify the God who motivated their makers.
Every worker, regardless of how humble his
task, was to view work as a religious discipline.

A few years ago my wife and I visited a small
ship-building community near Glasgow. We
talked to a few people and then asked a middle-
aged woman for directions to the shipyard. She
told us that she was on her way there to work
on the evening shift and would take us herself.

On our way we passed several shipbuilders
who had just finished their daytime shifts.

▓ To review

Review the standard of your daily work
(even if you don't have paid
employment).

Does it honour God or is it slipshod?

Take the appropriate action.

▓ To meditate on

God loves to see enthusiastic workers.
'Always give yourselves fully to the work
of the Lord, because you know that
your labour in the Lord is not in vain'
(1 Cor. 15:58).
'Whatever you do, work at it with all
your heart, as working for the Lord, not
for men, since you know that you will
receive an inheritance from the Lord as
a reward. It is the Lord Christ you are
serving' (Col. 3:23,24).

Each one greeted the woman enthusiastically. They all knew her name, and she knew all of them by name too. There was a fun-loving quality about her personality, and her whole demeanor said, 'I'm enjoying life'.

'What's your job at the shipyard?' I asked. She stopped, took my arm and spoke to me in such a way that I was sure she was about to tell me something of enormous importance.

'What do I do?' she asked. 'I'm the one who cleans the ships.' Then, obviously impressed with the importance of her task, she added, 'And you know, nary a ship goes to sea until I say it's clean enough. It's my job to see to it that every bit of dirt is polished away. That's what I do.' I was impressed. She saw dignity in her labour and was proud of what she did because she viewed her work as a holy calling.

I can remember when the label 'Made in Japan' meant that a product was inferior, and when American-made cars were the most carefully crafted in the world. The Protestant work ethic once caused even the most common of industrial tasks to be undertaken with pride. Isn't it time we saw our jobs as God-given and became enthusiastic about them?

▦ Food for thought

➤ Choose one of the following passages: Nehemiah 4:6–23 or Proverbs 31:10–31.

➤ If you have chosen the Nehemiah passage, write down the ways in which the workers responded to the pressure.

➤ Could you do anything that would help you to deal with pressure more effectively?

➤ If you have chosen the Proverbs passage, write down the qualities (not necessarily the actions) of the 'wife of noble character'.

➤ Which of these qualities would you like to demonstrate more in your life?

▦ To consider

What is your attitude to your daily work (whether paid or not)?

_____

_____

How could you improve your attitude? (e.g. by accepting your tasks as God-given, by not complaining so much, etc.).

_____

Pray that God will help you to enjoy your work more.

I am responsible for the cleaning at another church I used to be at. I go in three days a week ... The responsibility I have is hard work and can be tiring. I need the strength of the Lord and His help. Cleaning is something I am gifted with and I thank God He has called me to this work.
Linda
Taken from a private letter to a friend.

An honest living

As I grew up, I was taught the importance of thrift in the lives of believers. I was told to take note of the parable of the talents and to imitate the servants who were commended by their master. If I did the best with what I had been given, I would be rewarded. If I did nothing, even what I had would be taken away.

Protestant preachers were once happy for Christians to make money, but not so keen for them to spend it. They thought money should be saved and invested to gain more wealth. This teaching has caused many Christians to become sombre and to regard with suspicion anyone who spends money on pleasure.

Several years ago I was invited to speak at a church in Las Vegas, Nevada, the gambling capital of America. I was met at the airport by a solid Calvinist preacher who proceeded to lecture me on the evils of gambling.

It was strange that this pastor drove me to the MGM Hotel, the primary gambling centre of the city. But apparently the low room rates encouraged people to stay and gamble. Since I did not gamble, I could enjoy luxury at a very low cost and, I suppose, have more money to give to missionaries. It seemed to make sense.

▓ To consider

What is your understanding of Matthew 25:29?

_____

_____

_____

_____

Prayerfully consider your response to gambling.

▓ To meditate on

Money must never become our god.
'Dishonest money dwindles away, but he who gathers money little by little makes it grow' (Prov. 13:11).
'The love of money is a root of all kinds of evil. Some people, eager for money, have wandered from the faith and pierced themselves with many griefs' (1 Tim. 6:10).
'Keep your lives free from the love of money and be content with what you have' (Heb. 13:5).

The next morning, while waiting for the pastor to pick me up, I decided to put just one quarter in a slot machine. To my surprise, I hit the jackpot! Quarters poured out, alarm bells rang and lights flashed wildly. I was joyfully gathering my winnings when I happened to see the preacher approaching! I just managed to pocket the last coin before he came in.

When I consider the incredible needs in the world, I have to conclude that gambling is an inappropriate use of God's resources. It can become an addictive practice which ruins people's lives. Money should be earned by rendering diligent service to others in the name of Christ. It should not come by chance and without honest labour.

If people are diligent at their jobs because they believe their work to be God-given, they will probably make money. If they invest it, they will probably make more of it. The obvious increase in wealth will assure them that they are God's elect which, in turn, will stimulate gratitude to God for His great salvation. The circle is complete in that the primary way to show gratitude to God is through hard work. How productive are you?

▓ To do

Ask God to show you if you're frittering money away, e.g. purchasing luxury items, shopping at the more expensive places, buying sandwiches instead of making them, leaving the heating on all day, etc. How could you cut back?

_____

_____

Do you feel guilty when you spend money on yourself?
Read 1 Timothy 6:17 and seek God about this.

▓ Food for thought

➤ Read Job 31.

➤ Work steadily through the sins that Job could have committed and check your life against them.

➤ Pray that God will help you to be completely open and honest in all your dealings with, and treatment of, others.

Would Jesus have entered a casino? Certainly he is concerned about the people who go there today. He made it clear that those who are well do not need a physician, but those who are sick, and that he did not come to call the righteous, but sinners to repentance. It seems clear that the one who ate and drank with publicans and sinners would not have hesitated to conduct a search-and-rescue mission in a casino, or saloon, or house of ill fame.
John White

Blessed are the rich?

You know the grace of our Lord Jesus Christ, that though he was rich, yet for your sakes he became poor, so that you through his poverty might become rich (2 Cor. 8:9).

People today see nothing wrong with making a lot of money and are often willing to work hard to do so. But their motivation does not stem from deep-rooted religious convictions. It emerges from a self-centred materialistic philosophy which defines the 'good life' as something that rich people can buy. It's a worldly attitude that says, 'I want the things that seem to make life worthwhile.'

Someone once asked me if I thought that buying a BMW was a sin. Certainly, having a dependable vehicle is a legitimate desire, but there does seem to be something unchristian about spending the earth on a sports car. Would Jesus buy one if He were physically here? I doubt it. In the face of the desperate hunger and poverty in the world, I think that He would live simply and use His resources to help those who are simply trying to live.

I believe Jesus questions an affluent lifestyle in the presence of poverty. His parable about the rich man and Lazarus speaks volumes about His way of thinking. The rich man was dressed in fine clothing and ate sumptuous food while Lazarus, a beggar covered with sores, lay at his gate hoping for a few crumbs.

▓ To pray

Pray for people who are indifferent to the needs of others.

Pray also that the government will promote policies that benefit the poor more than the rich.

▓ To meditate on

The poor in Christ are actually rich. 'As servants of God we commend ourselves in every way ... poor, yet making many rich; having nothing, and yet possessing everything' (2 Cor. 6:4,10). 'Has not God chosen those who are poor in the eyes of the world to be rich in faith?' (James 2:5) 'I know your afflictions and your poverty — yet you are rich!' (Rev. 2:9)

When they died, Lazarus went to heaven, and the rich man to hell. The rich man wanted Lazarus to give him a drop of water but his request was denied. He then expressed concern about his brothers, which suggests that he was not bad in the way we view 'badness'.

His sin was not that he broke any of the Ten Commandments. He wasn't an adulterer, a thief or a murderer. In all probability, he came by his money through hard work. His sin was that he enjoyed a yuppie-like 'good life' while being indifferent about those around him who desperately needed help.

The New Testament writers make clear that God's elect are not really the rich. They are the people who have so responded to the needs of others that they themselves have become poor.

Once, my son and I were visiting our mission work in Haiti. As we walked down the streets of Port-au-Prince we were continually approached by begging children. I warned my son, 'Bart, if you give some of your money to these kids, they'll besiege you and not let you go until they've got every penny.' Bart simply glanced at me and answered, 'So?' Isn't that just how we should reply to such a warning?

▓ To consider

Read 1 John 3:17,18.

Pray for a deeper compassion for others and reach out to the poor whenever you have the opportunity.

Review the extent to which you are captivated by worldly pleasures.

▓ Food for thought

➢ Read the following verses and write down in a notebook:

- what they say about those who put their trust in riches

- how we should respond to such people.

Psalm 49;
Proverbs 11:28; 23:4,5;
28:6,11,20,22;
1 Timothy 6:9,10;
James 1:11; 5:1–6.

➢ Pray that you will not be led astray by the desire for worldly wealth.

The danger with going out to work and earning a living is that we can regard wages as ours by right. We may think, 'I worked really hard for this! I'll give God a bit, but this is mine because I earned it.' We've earned nothing except death, but we've received the gift of life. We've been set free from the world's money system to give and give and give. *Jackie Pullinger-To Frontline International magazine,* July/August 1993

Follow me

'If anyone would come after me, he must deny himself and take up his cross daily and follow me. For whoever wants to save his life will lose it, but whoever loses his life for me will save it. What good is it for a man to gain the whole world, and yet lose or forfeit his very self?' (Luke 9:23–25)

God identifies with the poor and oppressed in their sufferings and wants us to share His concern. His Kingdom is made up of people who are not out to accumulate wealth, but who confront the radical teachings of Christ and use their resources to meet the needs of the poor.

Many hard working Christians have some serious questions about just giving money away. They fear that the wrong kind of charity can be extremely destructive.

Every Christmas, church youth groups seek to demonstrate the Christmas spirit by making up food parcels for poor families. When they deliver these parcels, they are often surprised by the apparent lack of gratitude on the part of the recipients. They do not understand how humiliating it can be for the poor to be given food by a bunch of seemingly spoiled rich kids who regard them as inferior.

While we shouldn't stop giving Christmas parcels to the poor, we can change the way we operate. Rather than turn up with the gifts, it's a lot more fun to make the deliveries in secret.

Many believe that the best way of helping the poor is through job creation. At Eastern College we run a degree course which trains Christians

▓ To do

Pray for the poor in your community and in other parts of the world.

What could your church do to help them in the short and long term?

_____

_____

_____

_____

▓ To meditate on

There is a cost to following Jesus.
'Now if we are children, then we are heirs ... if indeed we share in his sufferings in order that we may also share in his glory' (Rom. 8:17).
'The sufferings of Christ flow over into our lives' (2 Cor. 1:5).
'It has been granted to you on behalf of Christ not only to believe on him, but also to suffer for him' (Phil. 1:29).
'Join with me in suffering for the gospel' (2 Tim. 1:8).

to mix with the poor and to help create cottage industries and small businesses. By financing economic development programmes, we hope to enhance the dignity of those we are helping and preserve their God-given humanity.

When we started the course, many said that we would never get young people to enrol on it. But they were wrong. We have discovered that there are scores of young people who refuse to be seduced into a yuppie lifestyle because they want to do something that will live on after them. They have realised that serving Christ sacrificially is more fun than anything the world has to offer.

When I met Mother Teresa, what impressed me wasn't her piety, but her smile. The instant I saw her, I knew that she was enjoying life more than any yuppie ever could. Once, when a famous television commentator interviewed her in Calcutta, he said, 'Mother Teresa, I wouldn't do what you're doing for all the money in the world.' And she answered, 'Neither would I.'

Jesus calls us to service that offers us the kind of fulfilment that the world cannot understand. To everyone who is thirsty for the joyful suffering of Christ, He says, 'Come!'

■ To consider

In what areas are you not completely following Jesus?

_____

_____

What are you going to do about this?

_____

_____

■ Food for thought

➤ Read Luke 14:12–14 and learn verses 13 and 14.

➤ In your sphere, who are the poor, the crippled, the lame and the blind? (e.g. the unemployed man down the road, the elderly woman who can't get out much, the single mum, the unpopular Christian, etc.).

➤ How could you put Jesus' words in Luke 14 into practice with these people?

➤ Wouldn't you enjoy the challenge?

In the passage where the New Testament says that everyone must work, it gives as a reason 'in order that he may have something to give to those in need'. Charity — giving to the poor — is an essential part of Christian morality: in the frightening parable of the sheep and the goats it seems to be the point on which everything turns.
C.S. Lewis

Job satisfaction

God saw all that he had made, and it was very good (Gen. 1:31).

'I was the craftsman at his side. I was filled with delight day after day, rejoicing always in his presence, rejoicing in his whole world and delighting in mankind' (Prov. 8:30,31).

People were overwhelmed with amazement. 'He has done everything well,' they said. 'He even makes the deaf hear and the mute speak' (Mark 7:37).

Everything God created is good (1 Tim. 4:4).

When my children were small, they enjoyed school most not when they had free time, but when they made things. It was always fun to welcome them home, have them hold up one of their precious creations, and hear them say proudly, 'It's for you'. The fun that my children had in their craft times prompts me to ask, 'Shouldn't all work be fun?'

My father used to be a cabinet maker. He worked for starvation wages, but got something from his job that was more important than money: gratification. He came alive when he fashioned things of beauty out of wood, and whenever he found one of his cabinets in use, he basked in self-satisfaction.

In Genesis 1, God expressed His personality through His creation and said that it was very good. Surely all human beings should be able to express themselves in their activities and experience a similar joy and satisfaction.

Job satisfaction is crucial for the success of family life. Someone who has to endure an emotionally draining and unfulfilling job is a lousy lover. If, at the end of a day, marital partners have a sick feeling that their lives are being wasted, they are unlikely to have much

▦ To do

Make a point of watching children enjoying themselves today.

Pray that you might catch their excitement for life.

▦ To meditate on

Heaven rejoices over God's works. 'Who laid (the earth's) cornerstone — while the morning stars sang together and all the angels shouted for joy?' (Job. 38:6,7)
'The LORD ... will take great delight in you, he will quiet you with his love, he will rejoice over you with singing' (Zeph. 3:17).
'There will be ... rejoicing in heaven over one sinner who repents' (Luke 15:7).

enthusiasm about personal relationships. Countless divorces can be traced to vocational activities that leave people dehumanised and emotionally dead.

For many, depression is a daily experience. Depressed workers make statements like, 'I'm a nobody', 'Nothing I do really matters', 'I'm treated like dirt', 'I get no fun'. Such negative feelings have a devastating effect on family life. Nobody enjoys being with depressed people.

Someone once said, 'When the children tire of their games ... they turn to torturing the cat.' When children are no longer having fun, they become mischievous. The same is true of adults but instead of torturing the cat, they torture each other. The deadness that comes from unfulfilling work shows itself in exhaustion and often leads to adultery, abuse and other evils.

Too many people overemphasise working hard and accumulating wealth. There must be more to a job than a salary. Work must be fun. Why? Because it energises people and makes them capable of loving; because life is too short to be spent doing the absurd and meaningless; because there's something unchristian about despising your employment. Don't you agree?

▓ To consider

f you are married, consider the effect that work (or the lack of it) is having on your family relationships. What is God saying about this?

_____

_____

f you are unmarried, pray that God will help married couples to overcome job tensions.

Pray for Christians who are doing unfulfilling work and or the unemployed.

▓ Food for thought

➤ Read Job chapters 38—41.

➤ Try to enter into the joy that God experiences as He reviews His creative work.

➤ Consider the satisfaction that Jesus must have had as He reached out to people.

➤ Praise Him that He rejoices over you.

In every person is the creation story. Since the first day of our beginning, the Spirit has brooded over the formless, dark void of our lives, calling us into existence through our gifts until they are developed. And that same Spirit gives us the responsibility of investing them with Him in the continuing creation of the world. Our gifts are the signs of our commissioning, the conveyors of our transforming creative power.
Elizabeth O'Connor

It's attitude that counts

Therefore, if anyone is in Christ, he is a new creation; the old has gone, the new has come! (2 Cor. 5:17)

Conversion involves far more than simply accepting doctrinal truths about Jesus. It is about enjoying a personal relationship with Someone who wants you to be transformed into His image. You begin to see the world through His eyes and to think and feel as He does.

The events you once saw in one way, you now view differently. So the job that didn't excite you because it was lowly and poorly paid suddenly becomes a channel through which you can serve others.

While Christopher Wren was directing the construction of St. Paul's Cathedral, he stopped to talk to a labourer who mixed cement. 'What do you do?' he enquired. Not realising that this was the great architect, the man replied, 'Sir, can't you see? I'm building a great cathedral.' Someone else might have grudgingly said, 'I mix cement — not much of a job, but it's a living.'

A woman was offered a job: to visit the new families in her district and inform them about the local community. She took it because she was a single mother who needed flexible hours, but the work often depressed her. She had been deserted by her husband and her visits to intact families reminded her of her loss.

■ **To consider**

How do you speak about your job/current situation?

_____

_____

Is this helpful or not?

_____

_____

■ **To meditate on**

Attitude is important to God.
'You were taught, with regard to your former way of life, to put off your old self ... to be made new in the attitude of your minds; and to put on the new self' (Eph. 4:22–24).
'Your attitude should be the same as that of Christ Jesus' (Phil. 2:5).
'Since Christ suffered in his body, arm yourselves also with the same attitude' (1 Pet. 4:1).

One day she became a Christian and her attitude towards her job completely changed. Instead of viewing it only as a necessary means of paying the mortgage and feeding her family, she began to see that it opened up all kinds of possibilities for Christian service. She was often involved in counselling and was sometimes able to share her testimony. She was also able to direct people into the ministries of the various churches in the community. This woman did not change jobs; she changed attitudes.

Unfortunately, conversion does not always make us happy in our work. Each of us is different and has unique gifts which, in turn, create unique interests. A particular job may offer great possibilities for Christian service and creative work, but the person in that job may not be made for it. It is easy to be misplaced and to end up in a job that is not for you.

The biblical way to personal fulfilment and a fun-loving approach to life stands in marked contrast to what the world prescribes. The world tells us that satisfaction comes through hard work, lots of money and financial security. The Bible says that it comes to those who do God's work through serving others.

▓ To reflect

Read Romans 5:3 and 1 Peter 4:13.
What should be your attitude in difficulties?

Is your attitude to your present circumstances worldly or godly?

Consider what potential there is in your current situation that you have not yet exploited.

▓ Food for thought

➤ Read Luke 12:15–21.

➤ What do you understand by the term 'all kinds of greed' (v.15)?

➤ Write down some examples of this.

➤ If you had met this man just after verse 17, what exactly would you have advised him to do?

➤ Is your focus on getting or on giving?

A Chinese pastor (was) imprisoned for his faith ... (and) the authorities ... gave him the very worst jobs to do. His main employment was cleaning out the human refuse tank whose contents were used for fertiliser ... To do this he had to get inside the tank. But he loved his job. For eighteen years he worked 'as ... for the Lord' (Col. 3:23). He found that because the smell was so overpowering, no one would come near him ... So he was able to sing gospel hymns at the top of his voice and no one would shut him up ... that human cesspit became his garden where he worshipped as he worked.
Ralph Turner

Self-service or self-giving?

'God so loved the world that he gave his one and only Son, that whoever believes in him shall not perish but have eternal life' (John 3:16).

I f we are created in the image of a God who enjoys His creative work, then you could argue that we should enjoy our work too. If we don't enjoy it, we are somehow denying part of what we are supposed to be.

God is a self-giver; He sent Jesus to die for us. A good job allows us the privilege of self-giving. The people who sacrifice themselves for others are fulfilling God's design for their lives.

For years an insurance salesman viewed his clients only as a means to make money. But when he became a Christian, his attitude changed and he began to view his work as an opportunity to serve others. After selling a policy, he continued to express loving concern towards his clients. As he turned his job into a mission of self-giving, he began to know job satisfaction as never before.

A young woman who was suffering from bad depression went to a psychotherapist but failed to respond to therapy. The psychotherapist was about to give up on her when she surprised him by bouncing into his office one day, her face aglow with excitement.

She explained that on the way to her therapy appointment her car had broken down. Her

▓ To do

Write down the names of two Bible characters who served themselves and two who served others. Alongside each name, write down one example to prove your point.

_____

_____

_____

_____

▓ To meditate on

God wants us to serve others.
'Be dressed ready for service and keep your lamps burning' (Luke 12:35).
'The greatest among you should be like the youngest, and the one who rules like the one who serves' (Luke 22:26).
'Serve one another in love' (Gal. 5:13).
'Each one should use whatever gift he has received to serve others' (1 Pet. 4:10).

pastor agreed to take her but needed to make a few hospital calls en route. When they arrived at the hospital, he suggested that she visit some of the patients. She encouraged and prayed with several of them, and they were immensely grateful for her concern. Self-giving service gave her an emotional lift.

When her therapist pointed this out she said, 'You don't expect me to do that every day, do you?!' She knew how to overcome depression and to make her life fun, but refused to do it. Serving others was too much trouble for her.

An accountant was depressed because he hated his job. To get a change of scene, he accompanied me on a brief trip to the mission field and helped the missionaries with their numerous accounting problems. As he sorted out the messes his face radiated with joy.

At the end of our stay he was reluctant to leave and the missionaries pleaded with him to join them permanently. His wife would have been thrilled to go with him, but he did the 'reasonable thing'. He rejected what would have made him a happy person and returned to the yuppie job that he despised. Few things are as unreasonable as that.

▓ To consider

Read Hebrews 12:2. How did Jesus serve us?

_____

Do difficulties mean that you must leave your job/ other situation? Give reasons for your answer.

_____

_____

_____

▓ Food for thought

➢ Read Genesis 24 and write down in a notebook the characteristics of Abraham's servant.

➢ Compare your own service with his.

People do their work in a grudging manner. They would prefer not to do it, and they wish they had not got to do it ... it has to be dragged out of them, as it were. The Apostle (Paul) says that we are not to work in that way, but always 'from the heart', from the soul, from the depth of our being. We are to be 'all out', and to show that whole-heartedness. 'Whatsoever thy hand findeth to do, do it with thy might' (Eccl. 9:10).
D. Martyn Lloyd-Jones

Don't you recognise me?

S erving others is the ultimate way for Christians to achieve joy and fulfilment. When I serve someone who needs my help, I sometimes have a mystical sense that Jesus is reaching out to me through that individual. When I touch them, I touch Him — that's why serving others is such a blessing.

During World War 2, the Nazi SS Troops sentenced all the Jews in a vicinity in Poland to death. The Jews dug themselves a shallow grave, stood beside it and were machine-gunned until they fell in. Their corpses were then covered with dirt. Among them was a ten year old boy. His naked body was splattered with blood, but none of the bullets hit him, so he pretended to be dead, fell into the grave and was buried with the rest. Fortunately, the thin layer of dirt still allowed him to breathe.

When darkness fell, he clawed his way out of the grave, limped to the nearest house and begged for help. Recognising him as one of the Jewish boys marked for death, the woman who answered screamed at him to leave and then slammed the door. Again and again he was turned away. The fear of helping him overcame any compassion that people might have had.

▩ To question

What do you think was the goal of Jesus' life?

―――――――――――――――――

What is the goal of your life?

―――――――――――――――――

Are you actually living for it?

―――――――――――――――――

▩ To meditate on

God is compassionate.
'The Lord ... has compassion on all he has made' (Ps. 145:9).
'Because of the Lord's great love we are not consumed, for his compassions never fail. They are new every morning; great is your faithfulness' (Lam. 3:22,23).
'... the Father of compassion and the God of all comfort, who comforts us in all our troubles' (2 Cor. 1:3,4).
'The Lord is full of compassion and mercy' (James 5:11).

At the next house, he said to the woman who opened the door, 'Don't you recognise me? I'm the Jesus you say you love.' She paused, then swept him into her arms. From then on, he became one of the family.

Wealth does not deliver the gratification that many of us think it will. It may be good to want to make money with a view to giving it away. But I believe that there is a better goal. When you can see your work as a means of helping others, you will have more fun at what you do.

Working for personal satisfaction certainly appears a reasonable thing to do. But I think that in most cases, those who seek it never really find it. Personal happiness is rather like a dog's tail. If the dog chases it, he goes round in circles. but if he goes purposefully about his business, the tail just follows along behind.

Strange as it may seem, people have fun if they forget what they will be paid and their longings for happiness, and give their lives for others. I believe that to live for Christ is to gain the joyful aliveness and fulfilment that the world so desperately seeks but never finds. There may be a lot of pain and sacrifice in serving Christ, but there's a lot of fun in it too.

■ To consider

How did Jesus express compassion?

In what areas would you like to see the church expressing compassion for others?

Do an act of compassion for someone this week and consider whether God wants you to be more involved in reaching out to others in the future.

■ Food for thought

➤ Read Luke 10:25–37.

• Look closely at the sequence of events from verses 33–35.

• Is there anything that the Samaritan failed to do?

• At which point would you have pulled out?

➤ Consider your response to the needs of those around you.

➤ Are you 'doing likewise' or getting away with the barest minimum?

The Christian understanding of work as self-fulfilment through the service of God and neighbour should have several wholesome consequences. We shall value our own work more highly; see to it that those we may employ are able to do the same; feel deeply for the unemployed, and try to ensure that though out of employment they are not out of work. In summary, all of us should expect to remain workers all our lives, so that even after we have retired, we may spend whatever energy we have left in some form of service.
John Stott

The importance of ritual

'Go at once and select the animals for your families and slaughter the Passover lamb. Take a bunch of hyssop, dip it into the blood in the basin and put some of the blood on the top and on both sides of the door-frame. Not one of you shall go out of the door of his house until morning' (Exod. 12:21,22).

We turn now from the workplace to the family. The divorce statistics suggest that building successful families is an increasingly difficult job. Our problems will not be solved by the mere statement that we must return to godly family values. We must actively figure out what we can do to establish the kind of healthy families in which people can have fun.

Emile Durkheim, the sociologist, taught that ritual is vital for the health and maintenance of any social institution. He claimed that ritual does four things for a group: it enhances group solidarity, builds loyalty, communicates the values of the group to new members and creates a strong sense of well-being.

Durkheim's theories are particularly relevant to the family in that ritual will generate greater solidarity which should promote happiness. His views suggest that families with high levels of ritual will have more stable marriages and healthy children than those with low levels.

Jewish families are steeped in traditional rituals. Their major holy days are not held as much in the synagogue as in the family. For instance, the Seder feast is celebrated in the home with the expressed purpose of teaching

▓ To do

Look up the word 'ritual' in a dictionary and write down what it means.

_____

_____

When do rituals become legalisms?

_____

_____

▓ To meditate on

God values family relationships.
'"I hate divorce," says the LORD God of Israel' (Mal. 2:16).
'If anyone does not provide for his relatives, and especially for his immediate family, he has denied the faith and is worse than an unbeliever' (1 Tim. 5:8).
'Marriage should be honoured by all, and the marriage bed kept pure, for God will judge the adulterer and all the sexually immoral' (Heb. 13:4).

the children about the slavery and deliverance of the Jews. Each of the foods is symbolical and through the ritual, Jewish children grow up knowing about ther roots and learning to be loyal to their ethnic brothers and sisters.

Jesus understood the importance of ritual and He used it well to maintain the values and truths essential for the survival of His Church. Central to His mission were His death and resurrection. Crucial to His Church is the remembrance of His saving acts of grace.

Because of the importance of these things, Jesus did more than exhort His followers to remember His death until He returned in glory. Instead, he wrapped up the memory of the cross in the ritual of communion. Whenever Christians celebrate the Lord's Supper, they are reminded of His sacrifice for them.

Jesus was asking for literal obedience when He declared, 'This is my body given for you; do this in remembrance of me' (Luke 22:19). He knew that if His followers did not ritualistically celebrate the Lord's Supper, they would be likely to forget the meaning of His death. In addition, the frequent repetition of the ritual would keep the cross central in their theology.

➤ Read Matthew 26:17–30 and 1 Corinthians 11:23–34.

➤ How could you make communion more meaningful/ interesting but not gimmicky? For example, get someone to speak to your housegroup about the Passover, include the breaking of bread in the context of a meal, watch the Lord's Supper scene in a video about Jesus and then take communion, go out as a group and take communion in the park, etc.

➤ Spend some time considering the meaning of Jesus' death for you.

➤ Think of a way in which you could express your gratitude to Him today, and put it into practice.

▓ To consider

Write down what for you are unhelpful rituals (religious or not).

_____

_____

Apart from communion, are there any New Testament rituals? If so, what are they?

_____

_____

Tradition gives me a feeling of solidarity and roots ... this generation finds itself sorely in need of meaningful moments that will strengthen relationships and build up moral muscle in our society. We need healthy memories of the past for a clear sight toward the future.
Gloria Gaither

Family rituals

One man considers one day more sacred than another; another man considers every day alike. Each one should be fully convinced in his own mind (Rom. 14:5).

S ome families like to follow rituals. They have set ideas on how to celebrate holidays and birthdays, and have certain expectations about behaviour and conversation at meals.

These families are usually the most secure. They seem to communicate more effectively to their children the values and truths which they believe to be most significant. They have proportionately fewer juvenile delinquents, and their children are psychologically more healthy. Rituals are good for the family, and instituting them makes family life more fun for everyone.

Take Christmas with the Campolo family, for example. On Christmas morning our children used to wake up early and want to open their presents. This was not allowed until later. They could play with the little things that we stuffed in socks and hung by their beds, but they had to wait until we had all eaten breakfast before they could get to the 'good stuff'.

After breakfast, we would sit in the living room, and Bart, our youngest, would pick up a present from under the tree and give it to my wife, who would read the tag aloud. Bart would then give it to the right person who would slowly open it while the rest of us cheered and

▓ To review

Review your seasonal rituals (birthdays, Christmas, Easter, public holidays, summer holidays, etc.)

Seek God about making some changes that will make these events more fun.

▓ To meditate on

God uses ritual to remind His people. 'My rainbow ... will be the sign of the covenant between me and the earth' (Gen. 9:13).
'Every male among you shall be circumcised ... and it will be the sign of the covenant between me and you' (Gen. 17:10,11).
'The Israelites are to observe the Sabbath, celebrating it for the generations to come as a lasting covenant' (Exod. 31:16).

guessed what it could be. We would go through the same ritual with all the presents.

Our gift-opening sometimes took hours. It is sad that children are allowed to dive straight into their presents and end the surprises of Christmas in just a couple of minutes. They miss the drama that ritual can create.

Of course, one day rituals must come to an end, and that's usually painful. Children leave home and get married and a new era begins. The parents become grandparents and enjoy new rituals with their enlarging family.

Ritual reminds us of the past. It helps us to recall feelings that we might otherwise forget. The wedding ritual means the most to me. When I marry people, I try to persuade them to use the traditional form of service. This is because weddings are not simply for the two people getting married. They are also for the married people who are watching and renewing their marriage vows at the same time.

As a boy in an Italian family, I had to attend countless weddings and funerals — which were great fun. I believe that I was affected by my constant participation in those ceremonies. They played a large part in forming who I am.

▓ To do

What rituals could you abolish/adopt that will make your life more satisfying/fun? (e.g. stop sleeping in on a Saturday and doing something worthwhile; stop putting things off and start doing them).

_____

_____

Devise a personal and specific plan of campaign (e.g. one Saturday a month I will ...).

_____

▓ Food for thought

➢ Read the following verses and write down in a notebook the things that we do well to remember.

Psalm 42:4,6; 77:11; 105:5; 106:7; 119:52,55; 143:5;
Matthew 5:23,24;
John 15:20; 16:4;
2 Corinthians 9:6;
Galatians 2:10;
Ephesians 2:11,12;
2 Timothy 2:8;
Hebrews 13:3,7.

➢ Look back at some of the milestones in your life and consider how you have changed.

➢ Spend some time praising God for what He's done in your life.

I went out and bought a big magnifying glass and said to the kids, 'Let's all go to the beach' ... We ... found all kinds of crabs, bugs, and other weird things. It was about an hour and a half of sheer excitement with the kids, just jabbering, talking, and sharing. And at the same time I was able to relate it all to God's creation and talk about how He made every living creature unique ... another memory they won't ever forget.
Josh McDowell

Family devotions

Blessed is the man who fears the LORD, who finds great delight in his commands. His children will be mighty in the land (Ps. 112:1,2).

An atheist once said to me, 'The family that prays together stays together, even if there is no God.' While he did not believe that there is a God who hears prayer, he was convinced that regular family devotions build family solidarity. He also believed that such rituals as prayer and Bible study provided one of the most effective means for encouraging children to commit themselves to the basic values of Christianity.

Christians need to take note of the unbiased observations of my atheistic friend. Children seldom learn from such direct approaches as lecturing or admonishing. I can remember telling my son, in no uncertain terms, why his failure to tidy his room each day would lead to his downfall. While I lectured him on the importance of personal responsibility, he sat with his head bowed and his eyes fixed on the cat. He then said meekly, 'Can I leave now?' And I realised that nothing I said had sunk in.

Family rituals, on the other hand, have the effect of committing children to family values. Children from families where ritual plays a large part have an intense longing to identify with their families and to do what their families see as right. Parents may want their children to

▓ To pray

Pray that Christians will know how to use family ritual so that it makes family life more fun.

Pray that the constructive use of ritual in the family will challenge unbelieving friends and neighbours.

▓ To meditate on

We must beware of unhelpful traditions. 'They ... followed the practices of the nations the LORD had driven out before them' (2 Kings 17:8).
'You have let go of the commands of God and are holding on to the traditions of men!' (Mark 7:8)
'See to it that no-one takes you captive through hollow and deceptive philosophy, which depends on human tradition and the basic principles of this world rather than on Christ' (Col. 2:8).

be loyal to family beliefs. But if those parents fail to have regular family devotions, they may discover that their children drift away.

Sometimes parents try to justify not having regular family devotions by saying that their children are not keen to participate. I point out that people do not have to like a given ritual for it to have a positive effect on them.

I do not want to convey the impression that disliking ritual is a normal reaction among children, for the opposite is true. Most children enjoy family rituals, particularly those of a religious nature. That's because family rituals help them to feel secure. They may have had a terrible day at school but be unprepared to talk about it. A ritual prayer time before they go to bed can help to rebuild their shattered world and convince them everything is OK.

Parents ask me how they can help their children overcome insecurities, embrace right behaviour and feel good about themselves. I reply, 'Ritual!' Without ritual, children forget what they should remember, lose sight of what they should believe and fail to learn how to behave. We do well to discover its importance, not only in religion, but in all of life.

■ Food for thought

➤ Read Luke 11:1–13.

➤ How would you describe your prayer life?

➤ How do you want it to change?

➤ If you are married, consider what God is saying about your prayers with your partner/family.

➤ Over the next few days, read a good book on prayer and make some changes in your timetable so that you can pray more.

■ To consider

Read Psalm 46.
Where does our ultimate security lie?

_____

_____

How can you tell whether someone is trusting God?

_____

_____

The greatest legacy we ever could leave our children and their children is their seeing and knowing the importance and power of family prayer. Prayer should be, and can be, the spontaneous lifestyle of every Christian family.
Evelyn Christenson

Love in action

Love is patient, love is kind. It does not envy, it does not boast, it is not proud. It is not rude, it is not self-seeking, it is not easily angered, it keeps no record of wrongs. Love does not delight in evil but rejoices with the truth. It always protects, always trusts, always hopes, always perseveres. Love never fails (1 Cor. 13:4–8).

Rituals build solidarity, generate loyalty, create a sense of well-being and remind us of things that we must not forget. But rituals are no substitute for love. Without love, marriage is no fun, and neither is life.

Society today thinks that love is an irrational emotion that you cannot control. We are encouraged to believe that once we have fallen for someone, we can expect to live happily ever after. It is no wonder so many marriages fail.

While it is reasonable to say that feelings should accompany love, we must understand that love is maintained by hard work. The Bible tells us that it is something we are called to do. It is a commitment to do things for others that will help them to become more like God.

Greek philosophy teaches us that what people think and feel determines what they do. While this is true, it is also true that what we do influences what we think. If we decide to do loving things for others, our actions can generate loving feelings towards them.

Sometimes I counsel people who say they don't love their partners any more. I tell them that within a month, the feelings of affection and fun will return if they do two things:

▓ To do

If you are married, do the exercise mentioned in today's study for at least a week.

If you are not married, do something each day for a week for people you do not naturally warm to.

▓ To meditate on

We must listen to others.
'A wise man listens to advice' (Prov. 12:15).
'He who answers before listening — that is his folly and his shame' (Prov. 18:13).
'Stop listening to instruction ... and you will stray from the words of knowledge' (Prov. 19:27).
'Everyone should be quick to listen (and) slow to speak' (James 1:19).

1. Make a daily list of ten things that they would do for their partner if they were in love.
2. Each day, do all of them.
There is no secret formula, just the age old truth that those who do loving things will have loving feelings.

When the Bible tells husbands to love their wives, it is exhorting them to love like lovers. If husbands do what lovers do, they will begin to feel what lovers feel. Love is about committing yourself to doing things for another person that will make that person happy. The more you do loving things for your partner, the more you will enjoy him or her.

Few things help foster feelings of love as much as attentive listening. Many men become preoccupied with other things, treat their wives with indifference and stop listening to them. Their wives find it hard to respond to someone who shows no genuine interest in them.

When people came to Jesus, He listened to them and responded to their requests. Love is about listening to others and acting on their behalf. It requires commitment, concern and concentration. Such love may not be easy, but it has a fabulous payoff.

▓ To consider

What evidence is there in the Bible that love involves hard work?

_____

_____

Evaluate your listening skills — preferably by asking someone else to give you his or her opinion of how well you listen.

Pray that you will become a better listener and work at this.

▓ Food for thought

➤ Read through Psalm 103.

➤ Read each benefit in turn and write down in a notebook personal experiences which bear it out (i.e. when the Psalm speaks of forgiveness, list some of the sins that God has forgiven you; when it speaks of healing, note what He has healed; when it speaks of your being redeemed, recall the way He led you to Himself, etc.)

➤ Over the next few weeks, why not do what D.L. Moody did (see quote)?

I took up that word Love, and I do not know how many weeks I spent in studying the passages in which it occurs, till at last I could not help loving people. I had been feeding on love so long that I was anxious to do everybody good I came in contact with. I got full of it. It ran out my fingers. You take up the subject of love in the Bible! You will get so full of it that all you have to do is to open your lips, and a flood of the Love of God flows out.
D.L. Moody

Power struggle

'The reason my Father loves me is that I lay down my life — only to take it up again. No-one takes it from me, but I lay it down of my own accord' (John 10:17,18).

'Greater love has no-one than this, that he lay down his life for his friends' (John 15:13).

The sociologist Willard Wallard, taught that for love to increase in a relationship, power must decrease. In his opinion. the person with the least love and least interest in maintaining a relationship will exercise the most power and control over it. Conversely, the person with the most love and most interest in keeping the relationship alive will be the most vulnerable and have little control over the other person.

Most of us have experienced this principle in our own lives. We know that painful, powerless, vulnerable feeling that comes from loving someone who does not return that love with the same intensity.

Some of us defend ourselves against such hurt by holding back on love. We recognise that love makes us vulnerable and become reluctant to take the risks that love requires. So we repress our feelings and hold back affection until we are sure of where we stand.

If we want to grow in love, we must voluntarily surrender power. This principle is best illustrated by Jesus, who, in His desire to express His love for us, was willing to set aside His power, humble Himself, assume the role of a servant, and allow Himself to be put to death.

▓ **To review**

If you are married, review your attitude to your partner and the way you teach your children.

If you are not married, to what extent are you motivated by power rather than a desire to love?

▓ **To meditate on**

God calls us to submit to others.
'Everyone must submit himself to the governing authorities' (Rom. 13:1).
'Now as the church submits to Christ, so also wives should submit to their husbands in everything' (Eph. 5:24).
'Obey your leaders and submit to their authority' (Heb. 13:17).
'Slaves, submit yourselves to your masters with all respect' (1 Pet. 2:18).
'Young men ... be submissive to those who are older' (1 Pet. 5:5).

If you want to enjoy the fun of being in love, you must not seek to exercise your will over others and insist on having your own way. Rather, you must risk making yourself vulnerable and, like Jesus, become a servant.

This important condition for love naturally flies in the face of male chauvinism. The man who demands to be in a position of domination reduces his capacity to express love. It is little wonder that so many men in the West find it difficult to say the simple words, 'I love you' in a meaningful way. Until the power of love becomes greater than the love for power, you will have little hope for a fulfilling relationship.

Women are often oppressed because men are on power trips. This may be because we train boys to be tough and aggressive. The more we encourage boys to love power, the more we will create men who lack the compassion and humility that are essential for loving.

Ideally, marriages should unite people who are prepared to 'submit to one another out of reverence for Christ' (Eph. 5:21). A husband and wife should be saying to each other, 'I will sacrifice all my dreams for you.' and learning to outdo one another in service and humility.

▧ Food for thought

➤ Read the following verses and write down in a notebook what God does for the person who is humble.

2 Samuel 22:28;
Psalms 18:27; 25:9;
147:6; 149:4;
Proverbs 11:2; 15:33;
22:4;
Isaiah 66:2;
Daniel 10:12;
Matthew 18:4;
Luke 1:52; 14:11;
1 Peter 5:5,6.

➤ What are the characteristics of a humble person?

➤ Do you qualify?

▧ To consider

Read Hebrews 5:7.
Why was Jesus heard?

_____

_____

What do you understand by submission?

_____

_____

Ask God if you are rebelling where He wants you to submit.

Do you really want to see divine power at work? Then discard your human notions of power and look at the way Christ lived and died.
Edmund A. Steimle

The church can have fun

God placed all things under his feet and appointed him to be head over everything for the church, which is his body, the fulness of him who fills everything in every way
(Eph. 1:22,23).

His intent was that now, through the church, the manifold wisdom of God should be made known to the rulers and authorities in the heavenly realms, according to his eternal purpose which he accomplished in Christ Jesus our Lord
(Eph. 3:10,11).

After being tucked into bed for the night, a small boy cried out, 'Mommy, I'm afraid to be alone in the dark. I want somebody to stay with me.' His mother responded, 'Don't be afraid. God is with you.' The little boy then said sadly, 'I want somebody with skin on his face.'

Two thousand years ago, the eternal Christ expressed Himself in a historical human body. His hands were those of God and through them God touched the lepers, the blind, the deaf and the dumb and made them whole. Jesus' feet were the means by which God walked among us and His tongue was the instrument through which God spoke the most important words ever put into human language.

God still seeks to manifest Himself in history, but the vehicle He uses is now the church. Through the church He wants to heal the sick, bring good news to the poor, establish justice and declare His gospel.

Jesus binds believers together and calls them to be the incarnation of His love, His body on earth. To be a Christian is to be committed to the church. People deceive themselves if they think that they can be Christians while refusing to participate in the body of Christ.

▨ To consider

Read 1 Corinthians 12:27.
Consider your commitment to the local church and let God speak to you about your involvement or lack of it.

Pray for a greater degree of joy in your church.

▨ To meditate on

God reaches others through His church. 'Then Peter said, "Silver or gold I do not have, but what I have I give you. In the name of Jesus Christ ... walk." Taking him by the right hand, he helped him up, and instantly the man's feet and ankles became strong' (Acts 3:6,7).
'(God) has committed to us the message of reconciliation. We are therefore Christ's ambassadors, as though God were making his appeal through us' (2 Cor. 5:19,20).

Now and again, someone reminds me that the church is full of hypocrites. In response, I say, 'That's why everyone is welcomed.' I have never met a person who was not to some degree a hypocrite, although many make the claim that they are not.

If you put a high value on being part of the church, you are valuing what can bring you joy and fulfilment. When the Holy Spirit began the church at Pentecost, God's people were so filled with excitement and joy that the onlookers thought they were drunk. But they were only experiencing the first real joy — the first real fun — that God had planned for His church.

People who refuse to be part of the church do not have the opportunity to enjoy the unity, the spiritual energy and joy that the Holy Spirit imparts to the body of Christ. But what if you feel that there is little joy in your church, if you see it as boring and legalistic?

Well, let me encourage you to be the person who brings the joy back. You can make a difference. You can express such enthusiasm that you will transform a dull church into a company of people who become known, among other things, for their infectious joy.

➤ Read 1 Corinthians 12:12–31.

➤ Review your role in the body of Christ.

➤ Are you close enough to others to suffer and rejoice with them, or do you maintain a respectable distance?

➤ How could you inject more life into your local church?

➤ Which of the 'greater gifts' are you eagerly desiring (v. 31)?

➤ Pray that God's joy will come into your church in a new way.

■ To do

Write down three encounters that Jesus had with people and note how He loved them.

_____

_____

_____

_____

Pray that He will use you more as an instrument through whom He can share His love for the world.

We have coined an expression at our church ... 'where the Spirit of the Lord is, there is fun!' ... A serious question often asked at pastoral staff meetings is, 'Are we still having fun?' We know that if fun has departed then we are setting ourselves up for some tremendous momentum problems.
Steve Sjogren
Equipping the Saints magazine,
Spring 1993

Fishers of men

'Go into all the world
and preach the good
news to all creation'
(Mark 16:15).

'As you sent me into the
world, I have sent them
into the world'
(John 17:18).

A great persecution
broke out against the
church at Jerusalem,
and all except the
apostles were scattered
throughout Judea and
Samaria ... Those who
had been scattered
preached the word
wherever they went
(Acts 8:1,4).

I once heard a television preacher say that television is the most effective means for evangelism. He was wrong. Although preachers are important instruments for the proclamation of the Word, ordinary church members are the primary agents for evangelising the world.

To impress an audience (of say, 1,000) with this fact, I sometimes take a survey. When I ask 'How many of you became Christians because of ...' I tend to get this typical response:
a TV programme? — a couple of people.
a tract or religious radio show? — no one.
an evangelistic crusade? — a respectable few.
a Christian? — an overwhelming number.

Professional clergy often find that unbelievers set up barriers that make it hard to share the gospel. I once went into the barber's and was greeted by, 'Good afternoon' in a normal tone followed by the shout of 'REVEREND!' Everyone froze. *Playboy* magazines disappeared and mundane conversations began. How could I possibly talk about Jesus now? Ordinary believers would have had no such barrier.

Some Christians claim that you can share the gospel only if your lifestyle is consistent with it. But if we had to be perfect to witness,

▓ To review

Review your attitude to witnessing and whether you could witness more.

Are you more conscious of your weaknesses than of Jesus' power?

Pray about this.

Give yourself a witnessing goal this week, then pray about it and do it.

▓ To meditate on

God delights to use weak material. 'The LORD said to me, "Do not say, 'I am only a child.' You must go to everyone I send you to and say whatever I command you"' (Jer. 1:7).
'God chose the foolish things ... to shame the wise ... the weak things ... to shame the strong ... the lowly ... and the despised things — and the things that are not — to nullify the things that are, so that no-one may boast before him' (1 Cor. 1:27–29).

who would ever qualify? Paul was not perfect but he preached Christ wherever he went.

Some Christians try to excuse themselves from witnessing because they feel inadequate. But God wants to use imperfect people to do His perfect will. Our effectiveness is dependent more on who He is than on who we are.

All God's people have been chosen to spread His Word and build His Kingdom. Many agree with this, but say that we must avoid straight verbal witnessing. 'We must live out the gospel' they say, 'then people will be influenced by our lifestyle and want to become Christians too.'

Well, I doubt that many people ask such Christians about Jesus. In fact, I think that most unbelievers are put off by those who suggest that they are better than others. In addition, I question whether many Christians have such a consistent lifestyle that others are impressed enough to want to be converted.

When I am preaching to people, I may sound like a 'super Christian' but I am all too aware of my flaws. I am committed to becoming more like Jesus every day, but while I am not yet perfect, I must preach a lifestyle that is better than the one I live — declaring Him, not myself.

➤ What Scriptures would you use to lead someone to the Lord?

➤ If you don't know, find out from a friend or a book.

➤ Now write them down in a notebook and learn the references so that when someone asks you how to become a Christian, you can turn to them without having to fumble around the whole of the New Testament!

■ To do

Pray by name for well known and local church evangelists. Ask God to make them effective in the proclamation of the Word.

Write down the area in your life where you most want to see change.

_____

_____

Pray about this and work on it all week. Expect to see victory.

TELL IT out! The message is too good to warrant silence. That the Lord is King is the secret of jubilation and blessing for all the world ... gladness becomes the saints. If the Lord Jesus has become King of your heart, and has brought blessing to you, do not hesitate to give voice to your allegiance. In private, sing unto Him a new song; in public, show forth His salvation, and declare His glory. Tell it out! Tell it out!
F.B. Meyer

Accept one another

Now the tax collectors and 'sinners' were all gathering round to hear (Jesus). But the Pharisees and the teachers of the law muttered, 'This man welcomes sinners and eats with them' (Luke 15:1,2).

My wife sometimes jokes that the church is the light of the world, and like all lights, it attracts bugs. She is not being unkind. Rather, she is simply saying that many strange people are drawn to the church because they would not be accepted by any other group.

Certainly some churches close their doors to people who are seen as socially inept. But many churches readily love such people and affirm the equal value of everyone in God's sight.

I am not trying to justify the church. When it comes to loving others, we all have much to learn. It's just that churches tend to accept people more readily than most social groups. Christians want to be as accepting as their Lord, and those who join them often say that one of the best aspects of being part of the body of Christ involves getting to know all kinds of people from different backgrounds.

When churches violate this principle of Christian hospitality, they are very likely to be denounced — not so much by the world, as by other churches. Even believers who have strong feelings against homosexual behaviour tend to agree that homosexuals themselves need loving acceptance, not fierce condemnation.

▓ To consider

Write down three examples that demonstrate how Jesus accepted people.

_____

_____

_____

To what extent do you accept others as Christ accepted you?

▓ To meditate on

We must learn to accept others. 'Live in harmony with one another. Do not be proud, but be willing to associate with people of low position. Do not be conceited' (Rom. 12:16). 'Accept him whose faith is weak, without passing judgment on disputable matters' (Rom. 14:1). 'Accept one another, then, just as Christ accepted you, in order to bring praise to God' (Rom. 15:7).

Several years ago I was asked to speak at a very formal and affluent Presbyterian church. The magnificent sanctuary, the stately worship and the properly dressed congregation blended together to give the impression that all things were being done 'decently and in order.'

Then suddenly the atmosphere was totally disrupted by a barefooted young man who was dressed in rags and spaced out on drugs. He stumbled down the main aisle to the front of the sanctuary and squatted on the floor by the pulpit. Everyone was taken aback.

Just then a tall, elderly gentleman dressed in establishment attire got up from his pew, walked towards the intruder, sat beside him and put an arm round his shoulder. They sat locked together for the rest of the service and 'preached' the real sermon that morning.

Loving acceptance has always been a primary factor in winning individuals to Christ. Hundreds of people will declare that it was not the piety of a church that challenged them to become Christians, but the love. No wonder ordinary believers tend to be more effective in the work of evangelism than the celebrated TV evangelists!

▓ To do

Read Acts 28:2,7 and reflect on the fact that the people mentioned here are welcoming prisoners.

What sort of people do you find it most difficult to accept?

Pray about this.

This Sunday, make a point of speaking to someone who is generally considered to be rather socially unaware. Why not invite him/her for a meal/coffee?

▓ Food for thought

➢ Read the following verses and write down in a notebook what they say about the sort of people that we should not welcome/ associate with.

Proverbs 22:24;
1 Corinthians 5:9–11;
2 Thessalonians 3:6,14,15;
2 John 7–11.

➢ How can we avoid having a judgemental attitude towards such people?

➢ What do you think about welcoming into your home those who belong to different cults?

➢ Is it wise to barter with them, 'If you come to my church, I'll go to yours'?

➢ Give reasons for your answer.

The designation 'sinners' as used by the scribes is roughly equivalent to 'outcasts.' The joint expression 'publicans and sinners' denotes well-known and despised classes among the people ... To the scribes Jesus' conduct was offensive because it was improper for a teacher of the Law to share meal fellowship with outcast and ignorant common people.
William L. Lane

Great expectations

For many Christians, worship meetings are boring. A great deal of the blame for this lies with those who lead them. If these people took worship seriously, I am certain that the attitude of many people toward Sunday worship could be transformed.

A lecturer in theology once complained to me that his students were almost indifferent to what happened in worship meetings. They put great emphasis on preaching, counselling, social action and pastoral visitation, but relegated worship to a place way down on the list of priorities. They forgot that the primary reason why believers meet is to worship God.

A friend of mine visited a local church. As she was leaving after the meeting, an older woman engaged her in conversation. While they were talking, the pastor's eight year-old son climbed into the pulpit and shouted over the public address system, 'Look everybody! Look at me! I'm in the pulpit.' The elderly woman who was talking to my friend remarked coldly, 'His father preaches that every Sunday.'

When pastors seek to glorify themselves, church ceases to be fun for anyone. The focus must be on God, and those who lead the

▓ To pray

Pray for the leaders, worship leaders and musicians in your local church.

Ask God to help them to seek His glory alone and to be sensitive to the moving of the Holy Spirit.

▓ To meditate on

Worship involves enthusiasm and joy.
'David ... danced before the LORD with all his might' (2 Sam. 6:14).
'I will praise you, O LORD, with all my heart' (Ps. 9:1).
'Clap your hands, all you nations; shout to God with cries of joy' (Ps. 47:1).
'Praise the LORD, O my soul; all my inmost being, praise his holy name' (Ps. 103:1).
'I will sing and make music with all my soul' (Ps. 108:1).

worship should spend hours planning and praying that people will be captivated by Him.

We are mistaken if we think that those 'up front' ultimately determine what happens in a worship meeting. All the people are supposed to be involved. Those who know this bring to the worship time an enthusiasm and expectancy even before they begin the first song. They turn an hour of worship into an hour of holy fun.

Several years ago, the pastor of our church died. He had led us for almost forty years and the church numbered about 2,000. I thought that he would be followed by an established preacher, and was stunned when the church appointed a young man who was fresh out of seminary. When I questioned the decision, I was told, 'Tony, we're goin' to make him great.' And they did. Their enthusiasm, support and prayer for that young man lifted him to a level of greatness that most preachers never reach.

Abraham Lincoln once said that people are usually just about as happy as they make up their minds to be. Christians have a choice when they meet together: either they can keep their expectations low, or aim to have a great time. It's obvious which Jesus would prefer.

▓ To question

What changes would you like to see in your services?

How could you contribute to these changes?

What do John 5:41–44; 8:50,54 and 12:43 say to you?

Are you responding appropriately?

▓ Food for thought

➤ How important is it to worship God in the way that the Bible describes?

➤ Read the following verses and write down in a notebook the expressions of praise that are missing in your local church.

Psalms 47:1; 89:1,2; 95:6; 134:2; 150:1–6.

➤ Is there any reason why your church should not be worshipping God in these ways?

➤ How long do you spend worshipping God each day? Do you express your private worship in biblical ways (singing, shouting, dancing, etc.)?

➤ Give reasons for your answer.

How is it possible to worship God publicly once each week when we do not worship Him privately throughout the week? Can we expect the flames of our worship of God to burn brightly in public on the Lord's Day when they barely flicker for Him in secret on other days? Isn't it because we do not worship well in private that our corporate worship experience often dissatisfies us?
Donald S. Whitney

The joy of service

I glory in Christ Jesus in my service to God (Rom. 15:17).

If anyone serves, he should do it with the strength God provides, so that in all things God may be praised through Jesus Christ. To him be the glory and the power for ever and ever (1 Pet. 4:11).

The church puts a high value on service. We serve Jesus by serving others and are committed to following His example.

Some people suggest that the world would be better off if missionaries stayed home and let the 'primitive' peoples live in the simplicity of their unspoiled cultures. But they fail to realise that some of the native customs involve child sacrifice, slavery and cannibalism. Whatever mistakes missionaries may have made, their motivation has almost invariably been love and concern for others.

Medical missionaries, William and Joanna Hodges, have faithfully served thousands of people in Limbe, Haiti. I visited the hospital at Limbe just after a revolution. There had been a breakdown of law and order, and many people were taking advantage of any opportunity to slip out of the country.

As William and I walked along, we were intercepted by two Haitian women who called to William, 'You do not think you can leave us, do you? We will not let you leave. You are our doctor. You belong to us. If you try to leave, many people will block your way.' 'I'm going to leave; just you wait and see,' he said jokingly.

▨ **To consider**

Read Mark 5:1–20 and write down the ways in which Jesus expressed love to a 'worthless' man.

_____

_____

_____

_____

Consider your response to euthanasia (mercy killing).

▨ **To meditate on**

We are precious to God.
'The LORD takes delight in his people' (Ps. 149:4).
'I was the craftsman ... delighting in mankind' (Prov. 8:30,31).
'Look at the birds ... Are you not much more valuable than they?' (Matt. 6:26)
'The Father himself loves you' (John 16:27).
'Cast all your anxiety on him because he cares for you' (1 Pet. 5:7).

'No! You cannot!' they shouted back. 'We will not let you. We love you too much to let you go.'

Haiti is shot through with poverty, and death is accepted as an everyday occurrence. In such a place, it would be easy to get the idea that life is not precious, but the Christian influence of the Hodges has kept this from happening. One day, as I toured the bleak wards of the hospital, I saw an amazing example of how precious life can be for those who are in Christ.

In one of the wards there was a thirteen year old hydrocephalic girl. Her brain had been compressed by fluid in her skull and for almost all her life, she had sat cross-legged on that bed nervously rocking her deformed body. The Christian nurses changed her diapers many times a day for years without complaint.

One day, she accidentally crashed to the cement floor and almost died. I thought that the tired nurses might welcome her death as God's will. But no. They prayed hard for her, cared for her and gave her back her life.

Society suggests that it is better to leave the 'inferior' forms of life to die. Jesus responds, 'Whatever you did for one of the least of these ... you did for me' (Matt. 25:40).

▓ To do

Are you trying to get out of something that God wants you to stay in?

Pray for missionary work in one particular country.

Write an encouraging letter to someone who is serving God abroad.

Consider whether God is calling you to go overseas to serve Him.

▓ Food for thought

➢ Meditate through Psalm 139:1–18.

➢ Learn the verse(s) that mean the most to you.

It is when we lose our joy that our strength seeps away. The joy of the Lord Jesus when He was here on earth never rested on the seeming success of His mission. It was not in fact attributable to anything outward, but only to His steadfast pursuit of the will of the Father — 'the joy that was set before Him'. Thank God that we do not have to try to copy Jesus, but only to keep our eyes on His goal. His joy is ours by the Holy Spirit.
Watchman Nee

Jesus shares our fun

Some Christians grit their teeth and make themselves do what has to be done in the name of Jesus. Others have discovered that serving Him is actually fun.

Mother Teresa does not get up in the morning and say to herself, 'Well, here goes another rotten day on the stinking streets of Calcutta.' She has discovered what must seem like foolishness to the world — the joy that comes from encountering Jesus in the suffering people that she cares for every day.

I have a hard time understanding why so many people buy into a cultural value system that promises fun and fulfilment to those who achieve positions of wealth and prestige. So many of these so called 'successes' have broken marriages, are on drugs or need psychiatric care. If they were honest they would admit that their self-centred lives are empty, not fun.

How hard it is to convice today's young people that they can have greater joy in serving others than in using a Golden American Express card! How crazy it must seem to them that they can get more kicks out of fixing up houses for poor families than out of buying the latest gadget! How contrary to society's thinking

▓ To pray

Pray for Mother Teresa's work in Calcutta.

Ask God to help the workers to reach out with the gospel as well as with practical support.

▓ To meditate on

Selfishness does not bring fun.
'Turn my heart towards your statutes and not towards selfish gain'
(Ps. 119:36).
'An unfriendly man pursues selfish ends'
(Prov. 18:1).
'Do nothing out of selfish ambition or vain conceit, but in humility consider others better than yourselves' (Phil. 2:3).
'Where you have envy and selfish ambition, there you find disorder and every evil practice' (James 3:16).

is the notion that there is more fun in giving than in getting!

There is much evidence that self-giving is what really makes people happy, but somehow most people ignore this evidence and allow themselves to be seduced by the world's values. In saddening reality, the vast majority reject the ways in which God has ordained that we have fun.

When my son was nine years old, I took him to an amusement park. All afternoon, we laughed and screamed until it was time to go home. Then he said, 'I think Jesus wants me to have one more ride on the roller coaster.' 'How come?' I replied. 'Well,' he said, 'in your sermons, you say that whatever we feel, Jesus feels. That means that when I'm having a good time, so is He. And I think that He would like another ride on the rollercoaster.'

I do not want to construct a biblical justification for my son's theology, but I must admit that there is some truth in what he said. If Jesus shares our emotions, then the more we enjoy life, the more He does. He has a vested interest in our happiness and invites us to do the things that give Him the greatest pleasure.

▓ To do

Make enquiries. Does someone you know need help? You supply it.

Do something that will give you physical pleasure this week, e.g. amusement park, cycle ride with friends, walk in the beach, sailing, football, fishing, etc.

When you get back, spend time praising God for the joy you had.

▓ Food for thought

➤ Read the following verses and write down what you learn from them about pleasing God.

Psalm 19:14;
Proverbs 15:8,26; 16:7;
John 5:30; 8:29;
Romans 12:1; 14:17,18;
1 Corinthians 7:32–35;
Galatians 1:10; 6:8;
Ephesians 5:10;
Colossians 1:10–12;
3:20;
1 Thessalonians 2:4; 4:1
1 Timothy 2:1–3; 5:4;
2 Timothy 2:4;
Hebrews 10:6–8, 38;
11:5,6; 13:16;
1 John 3:21,22.

Fun and laughter, originally designed by God to remove the friction of monotony from the machinery of existence, begin to be viewed as enemies instead of friends. Intensity, that ugly yet persuasive twin of hurry, convinces us we haven't the right to relax ... we must not take time for leisure ... we can't afford such rootless, risky luxury. Its message is loud, logical, sensible, strong, *and wrong.*
Charles R. Swindoll

Let's party!

'These who have
turned the world upside
down have come here
too' (Acts 17:6 NKJV).

One scene in the film, *Becket* really impressed me. Becket, who was about to become archbishop, was required to give away all his worldly possessions to the poor. The needy gathered in the cathedral and he distributed his wealth among them. Suddenly he stopped, turned towards the front of the cathedral, pointed at an image of Jesus and shouted, 'You! Only you know how easy this is.'

That, of course, is exactly what the world refuses to believe. People take one look at the requirements of discipleship and conclude that religious life is devoid of fun. 'Spirituality is boring' they think. 'I couldn't keep it up.' They fail to understand that there is joy in self-giving and that the gospel is a contradiction of the wisdom of this world.

Have you noticed that God requires His people to enjoy themselves? In Deuteronomy 14:22–27 He commanded the Israelites to set aside one tenth of their wealth each year and use it to celebrate His presence among them. Everyone was invited: rich and poor; holy and sinners; yuppies and social rejects; lame and blind. A God who throws parties must love seeing His people enjoy themselves.

▩ To do

Read John 12:3–8 and check your attitude towards people who 'squander' what could otherwise have been given to the poor.

How do you feel about Christians having holidays, enjoying new possessions, etc.?

Seek God about whether your attitude is as balanced as He would like it to be.

▩ To meditate on

God specialises in fulness.
'God sent his Son ... (so) that we might receive the full rights of sons' (Gal. 4:4,5).
'His body (is) the fulness of him who fills everything in every way' (Eph. 1:23).
'I pray that you ... may be filled to the measure of all the fulness of God' (Eph. 3:17,19).
'In Christ all the fulness of the Deity lives in bodily form, and you have been given fulness in Christ' (Col. 2:9,10).